Cover by John Gillis
Glasnevin Cemetery, Dublin, Ireland

Photos by Cheryl Lynn Carter

Whispers Beyond the Grave

Copyright © 2015 Cheryl Lynn Carter

ISBN - 13: 978-1515371496
ISBN – 10: 1515371492

Dedicated to

Elizabeth, Dakota & Rosco

Table of Contents

Introduction

Once upon a time in a small Midwest town, this little brown eyed girl was born. I was just an average child with wide-eyed innocence and curiosity. As I grew, that inquisitiveness expanded by leaps and bounds. But soon I came to realize how different I was from the other children.

It was because this little girl had a special secret. By no means was it something I could share with a friend; not a chance. Besides who would ever take me seriously? Would they believe dead people spoke to me and I spoke to them?

And so begins my story …

Whispers Beyond the Grave

Cheryl Lynn Carter

"Says she talks to angels.
They call her by her name.
Oh ya, she talks to angels.
Says they call her out by her name."

--- Black Crows

Chapter 1

Becoming Me

I fearlessly wiggled my way under the bed past a herd of wild dust bunnies. Deeper and deeper I made my way through the dark abyss searching endlessly; occasionally flinging one of Grandma's high heels or fuzzy slippers that hindered my way. I was destined to reach my buried treasure. Finally, having it in my grasp, I pulled out my little suitcase.

Grandma Alice was going to take me on a trip. I loved that suitcase with Snow White and the Seven Dwarves painted on the front. Nobody else in the neighborhood had one like that. Yes, I was already cool at the age of four.

Quickly, my little hands got busy gathering up all the necessities. Under my clothes, I hid some of my favorite story books just in case things got boring. Somehow I knew they wouldn't. Grandma said she wanted to check it out for me when I was finished. She didn't want to leave any important stuff home. I wasn't quite sure what important stuff a four year old would have, but Grandmas know these things. Before she even looked inside, she said, "You can just leave those story books home." Now how did she know that?

Having removed the story books and being satisfied with the packing, she gave it her seal of approval. Then she carefully lowered the lid and closed the latches. We were ready for our trip. I felt it was going to be an experience I would never forget.

The next morning, we went down town to the Grey Hound station. As Grandma handed the man her money, I tried to look over the counter. It was quite high and I had to stand on tip toes to see what was going on. As the man handed her the tickets, he pointed to where we could sit down. Looking around the room, I imagined there wasn't much for a little girl to do except look out the window and wait. Oh, it was so hard to wait.

I didn't enjoy being in the bus lobby. It wasn't much fun. The chairs were hard and there were those men smoking stinky cigars. *Phew!* And that man with the newspaper sitting next to me was thinking so loud. "Got to get out of this town. There's nothing here for me."

Oh, that was silly. You can't hear people think. But I didn't feel comfortable about it and decided to move to the other side of Grandma. And yet, for some reason, I could still hear that man. Even with my hands tightly covering my ears, I clearly made out. "Wish that bus would get here." *Me too!*

After appointing myself our official look-out, I stood guard by the window keeping a watchful eye out for our bus. Yet I couldn't help but glance back over my shoulder at the man pretending to read the newspaper. Try as I might, I just couldn't get his voice out of my head.

Luckily it wasn't too long before the bus pulled up to the curb. The man behind the counter announced, "All aboard for Rockford."

"That's us," Grandma said. As we stood in line, well Grandma did, I was nervously hopping around as I tried to imagine what it would be like today. The huge grin that reached from ear to ear was making my cheeks hurt.

I was a seasoned traveler having been on a bus many times before. Grandma would let me drop the coins into the slot. Plink. Plink. Of course, we only rode to the next town to go shopping. But this was different. There wouldn't be any coins today. Grandma had given the man some folding money to pay our way. This was serious business. And the bus looked so beautiful compared to the city ones. Yes indeed, it was going to be an unforgettable experience.

However, the smile on my face began to fade. I started to get a bit concerned as the man loaded our suitcases into the luggage compartment. We couldn't let anything happen to Snow White. As we engaged in a friendly game of tug-a-war, the driver promised me he would take good care of her. After squinting and giving him the best four year old evil eye I could muster, the suitcase was in his hands. I nervously twisted the bottom of my shirt and watched closely as he closed the compartment door.

Maybe we should check it. What if the door opens on the way? Can't I put Snow White under my seat? Grandma looked at me and explained that the man had locked the door and nothing would fall out; besides my suitcase would not fit under the seat. Then I could have been mistaken, but did the greyhound just wink at me? Perhaps he was letting me know everything would be all right. Dogs are smart that way. Yes, they are.

Soon we boarded and looked for our seats. To my surprise, they were soft and comfortable like the ones in our car. Well, I was right the city bus sure didn't compare to this one. We were so lucky; our seats were in the front. Grandma let me sit next to the window so I wouldn't miss a thing on the way.

As the bus with the big dog on the side headed down the street, I waved good bye to my little town. I watched closely and was enchanted as the scenery magically transformed from city streets to country roads.

Whenever we approached a railroad crossing, the driver stopped the bus, opened the door and looked down the tracks. *Why do we keep stopping? There aren't any people. We're never going to get there this way.* Grandma explained he was looking for trains. I gazed all the way down the tracks too and hoped there would be one coming, but we never saw one.

Being intrigued with the change of scenery, I absorbed every detail as we passed each farm with the same tall silo, weather vane and big red barn. I thought how remarkably similar the farms were to Brookfield Zoo. I loved to feed the animals. But unlike the zoo with the fierce lions and tigers, the farm animals were gentle. No, there was nothing scary about the farm.

We were on our way to visit my aunt and uncle. It was going to be so much fun. I wasn't sure why, but I seemed to have some sort of fascination with farms. It was almost as though it were a familiar place to me. The sights, sounds and smells made me feel as if I were returning home again. Now that was a peculiar thought for a young city child. Years later, I would come to understand this better.

The bus ride seemed to take forever even though in reality it was only thirty-five minutes. Of course, in a child's mind that was an eternity. The splendor of this magical journey was starting to fade. *Are we there yet?* I'm not sure how many times I asked that question. I only remember Grandma kept telling me, "Just look at the cows." And I, having an inquisitive way about me, obviously had questions. *Cows? I don't see any cows. Where are they?* Grandma would give me that look and say, "Well, they're out there. You just have to look."

Finally, the bus stopped at a gravel crossroad. Why were we stopping here? We were in the middle of nowhere. There weren't even any animals. The driver opened the doors and informed us that we had reached our destination. *No, I don't think so. My aunt does not live in a corn field!* Grandma looked out the window and waved to somebody. Sure enough it was my aunt.

The driver got out, opened the compartment to retrieve our suitcases and loaded them into her car. I carefully inspected Snow White before they closed the trunk and just as he promised, she was ok. I knew she would be.

I stared out the back window and watched as the bus traveled down the road. It got smaller and smaller until it disappeared over the horizon. We turned on to a gravel road and headed to the farm. Much to my surprise the smooth pavement of the highway had morphed into thousands of little rocks. It was a very bumpy ride. Pop, pop, pop. It sounded like Grandma's peculator.

A huge cloud of dust appeared behind us as the tires met with the dry gravel. The dusty smell filled the air. It made its way deep into my nose and made me sneeze. *Why is there so much dust out here? It stinks. I want to roll the window down.* Grandma gave me that look again. "Just look at the cows," she said. "See those brown ones? That's where they get chocolate milk."

As we continued along the winding road, the view became more pleasing to a four year old. Lucky me, at least now there was a multitude of animals to see. Not only were there cows, but low and behold we now had ducks, horses and pigs. Yes, there were pigs. Instantly, the fragrant bouquet permeated the air. I recall thinking the dusty smell wasn't that bad after all. *It stinks. Why does it stink so much?* Grandma shook her head and said, "Just hold your nose. Look, there are cows up ahead."

Squeezing my nostrils tightly I looked out the window and sure enough, there were more darn cows. And again being that overly curious child, I wondered. *Grandma, if we get white milk from the white cows and chocolate*

milk from the brown cows, what do we get from those spotted cows?
My aunt laughed so hard she almost spit out the gum she
was chewing. Had this not been a perfectly logical
question? Poor Grandma just shook her head.

Finally, we pulled into the driveway of my aunt's
farm. *Oh boy, there's a big barn, some tractors and a chicken house!*
I jumped out of the car ready to explore. "Hold your
horses," Grandma said, "We have to carry our suitcases
into the house first." Awe, that sure didn't sound like
much fun.

My aunt said if we hurried there would be lots of
time for fun. We all agreed and commenced carrying
everything upstairs where there were two rooms. This was
where we would be sleeping. How exciting, we didn't have
an upstairs at our house.

After everything was out of the car, Grandma said
I could finally go outside and play. We would go see the
animals tomorrow. That was all right with me since we
had already seen more than enough cows for my concern.
She told me to go into the backyard and play on the swing.
They were going inside to have some tea and coconut
cookies. *Yuck!*

I hurried as fast as possible and rescued the lonely
swing. It had been some time since it had enjoyed the
company of a young child. We were going to get along
famously. As we glided through the summer air, I leaned

back to look at the fluffy clouds above me. Maybe I would spy some familiar shapes in the sky. But just then, my train of thought was interrupted.

"Cheryl." I jumped off the swing and ran into the house. I asked Grandma what she wanted. She said she didn't call me. Feeling puzzled, I did an about face and headed back to the yard. No sooner had the swing taken flight, when I heard it again.

"Cher-yl," the voice said in a sing-songy way. That time I was sure Grandma was calling me. Stopping the swing in mid flight, I ran back into the house. Grandma insisted she did not call me. My aunt said that perhaps it was just the wind. Sometimes the wind makes strange sounds when you are out on a farm. *But it's not windy.* Reluctantly, I retreated to the yard.

I steadied myself on the seat once more, but did not move. Instead, my ears listened intently for the voice. There WAS a voice. Why wouldn't anyone believe me? Oh, that's right she's a four year old. One thing for sure, it was a voice that somehow sounded familiar to me. If it wasn't Grandma, who was it? I waited and hoped, but heard nothing. Who had been calling me? What did they want? Where did they go? It would be years later before I would fully understand.

The following morning when I awoke, Grandma had already gone downstairs. I crouched down, reached into Snow White and retrieved some clothes being careful not to disturb the rest. After getting dressed, it was time to begin exploring. Wonder what's in the other room?

It appeared the room next to me was used for storage. There were some old trunks and boxes stacked in various places. Maybe we could take a peek inside some of them. Nobody would ever know.

I took a few steps toward the room. The floor let out a little creak. Oh, no. If this secret mission were to be successful, the shoes had to go. Thinking this would make a difference, I carefully removed each one and set them gently on the floor. Slowly, like a ninja, I tip toed to the doorway in my stocking feet. Once inside I realized that for some reason the room had an eerie feeling. It was hard to explain, but the air in there seemed different than the bedroom.

I sneaked over to one of the old trunks, making sure not to let the floor creak and alert anyone to my mischief. The top was covered with dust. With my little finger, I reached up scrawling my name in my best childlike penmanship. Carefully, my fingers moved down the side and pulled on the two latches. Click! Click! The sound was a lot louder than expected. Hopefully, no one heard. After hesitating a few seconds, it seemed the coast was clear. I slowly started to lift the lid and peeked inside. What treasures would there be? Much to my disappointment the trunk was filled with hats. As much as

I liked playing dress up, this find was not going to meet my exploration expectations.

It began to feel cool around me much like the gust of cold you get when you open the refrigerator. That was very strange since it was the middle of summer. I glanced over to the doorway which seemed so far away. Had this been such a good idea? Oh well, too late now. We're already inside.

My eyes scanned the room in search of something more interesting. On the far side of the room, the ornate hinges on another trunk caught my eye. Surely there had to be something special in that one. Upon approaching the trunk, the energy around me changed. The hair on my arms was full of electricity. I looked up and was startled to see a small boy standing behind the trunk. He appeared to be a little older than me. He had dark hair and was wearing a blue long sleeve shirt and pants. I wasn't sure what to make of this since I could see right through him.

He reached for my hand and said, "Come play with me." His hand was cold and I jumped back. "It's ok. Come play with me," he said. As fast as my little legs would carry me, I made my escape to the other room hoping he would not follow me. Without looking back, I ran down the stairs two steps at a time to safety. Needless to say, that was all it had taken to satisfy my curiosity for a long time.

Never again would I enter that room. I could feel his presence every time I stood near the doorway. However, for some reason he wouldn't or couldn't cross the threshold. I sensed he had not been feeling well. His chest ached from all the coughing. I could see his mommy covering him with a warm blanket; he was so very cold. She gently kissed his forehead. "Sleep well, sweetheart," she said. "Hope you feel better soon." All I knew for sure was that he seemed all better now.

I never told Grandma or my aunt what happened. If they wouldn't believe the voice was real, how in the world were they going to take this? It was way too much to fathom. It would be many years later as a grown woman that I would finally tell my aunt about the mysterious little boy in her house.

And so what had started out to be an innocent trip to the farm, had in fact, ended up robbing me of my child-like innocence. I was no longer the same little brown eyed girl. What had happened out there was a mystery to me. Who would ever believe me? Surely, grown-ups would merely discount it as some sort of childish foolery. Yes, I would have to keep this secret to myself.

One of my favorite times was when Grandma would open up her cedar chest or as she liked to call it, her treasure chest. As she lifted the lid, the earthy scent of cedar filled the room. That was such a great smell. She reached inside and brought out some old books. As much as I adored Snow White and Cinderella, they paled in comparison to these.

Together we sat on the bed surrounded by generations of relatives living within the weathered pages. I watched as she carefully turned each page of black and white photographs fastened on with tiny black corners. Memories in bits and pieces spilled out before our eyes. Grandma said they were places she could return to again and again no matter how much time goes by. Although I did not know who these people were, it appeared they made Grandma smile. It was as though they were talking to her. Of course, that was silly. Pictures didn't talk.

I was hoping it would be possible for me to look through one of the books by myself. I would be careful. Grandma wasn't so sure that four year old fingers would be able to accomplish this feat. Instead, she handed me some pictures, known as Cabinet Cards that had been glued into cardboard folders. Discovering these to be images of children, I was delighted to get to know them.

Grandma said she needed to go into the kitchen to check on her bread in the oven. She reminded me to only look at the pictures in the frames and to be careful at that. She would be back in a few minutes. Then we would look at the books together.

Feeling proud about my new big girl privilege and wanting to prove my abilities, I meticulously arranged the folders on the bed. Within a tweed patterned frame, a baby girl sat on a wicker chair. She looked simply precious in her white lace dress and patent leather shoes. There was a darling little curl on top of her head. Her brother of about four stood by her side. He looked dapper in his jacket and knickers. And the string tie was just adorable. He was very proud to be the big brother and enjoyed taking her for a ride in his little red wagon. Carefully tucking her inside, he watched out for any bumps as he pulled the wagon down the sidewalk.

Wow, that was fun. Pictures do talk to you. It felt as if my hand was a telephone allowing me to connect to some unknown place without ever dialing the number. How could this be? I couldn't explain it. But I waved my finger like a magic wand and reached for another one.

Two girls about age seven were wearing white taffeta First Communion dresses signifying the purity of their young souls. They had big bows in their hair and prayer books in their hands. The girl with the short hair had a doll wearing a pretty pink dress made with rows and rows of ruffles. Her porcelain face was surrounded by big brown curls. She loved her dolly. The other girl was often mean to her for no reason. But because she was shy, she was afraid to speak up to her bully. The mean girl grabbed the doll and threw it. The pretty porcelain face cracked as it hit the brick sidewalk. The girl gathered up her dolly as tears rolled down her checks. The mean girl laughed and said, "Cry baby cry! Stick a finger in your eye!"

I didn't like that mean girl and quickly put the picture down. I wasn't sure who she was and didn't care to find out. Why would Grandma have a picture of a bad girl? It just didn't make sense. My eyes carefully studied the remaining pictures and were drawn to a frame with gold around the edges.

There was a one year old sitting on a rattan chair. A girl perhaps my age was standing next to him. What really stood out to me were her big brown eyes. Something about them scared me. Then it was as if an electrical current flowed from that picture into my hand. I could feel the madness she carried inside. She was so jealous of the baby who had taken the spot light away from her. Now she had to share her daddy and compete for his attention. But how would she be able to do that? It was all about the baby boy and she was not going to stand for it. Something had to be done.

She took the baby outside with the promise of feeding the ducks. Out by the pond, when nobody was watching, she grabbed the back of her brother's shirt and pushed his head into the water. Rage and resentment pulsed through her veins. Had it not been for her mother calling them to dinner, she might have succeeded. "Don't you dare tell!" the girl shouted to me.

Suddenly, the picture became so hot it almost burned my fingers. I dropped it and looked at my hand. Everything seemed all right. But it wasn't. I wanted those bad girls to go away. I never wanted to look at their faces again. Never, never, never!

Just then, Grandma returned from the kitchen. She gazed down at the pictures with a puzzled look on her face and asked me what had happened. Why had I scribbled on the faces of those two girls? *They're bad girls, Grandma, very bad.*

* * *

Often times I would go with Grandma to visit her friend Eleanor who lived up the street. Sometimes we would pass Mr. Carr, a gray haired man, on our way. I would wave to him and he always waved back. We shared a secret wink. There was something about him that only the two of us knew. How I became privy to this information I do not know. He would visit the lady across the street for tea. But oh, he was also kissing her. Sometimes he would visit the lady next door and kiss her too. His wife didn't have any idea what was going on. *That's ok; Mr. Carr your secret is safe with me.*

As we turned up Union Street, there was an old tree stump. It was not like your usual stump as it stood about eighteen inches tall. Every time we walked past there I got a weird feeling. *They need to cut that down. Somebody is going to hit their head.*

That day as we passed by, something strange happened to me. I saw a bright light that blinded me. My body jerked as if somebody had pushed me. Then my head hurt really bad. At the same time, the hoot owl sitting up in the tree across the road started to hoot over and over.

"Did you hear that?" Grandma asked. "When the owl keeps hooting that means something bad is going to happen. I can feel it coming." *Me too, Grandma, me too.*

The man stumbled out into the night. He fumbled with his car keys. After several attempts, his hand shaky from too much alcohol, succeeded in finding the ignition.

The twelve year old boy waved good bye to his friend. He promised his mom he would be home before the lightning bugs came out, but they got so involved in their game of Parcheesi that it was now dark; very dark. Luckily he only had to cross the street.

The engine roared as the car barreled up the hill savagely piercing the darkness. The last thing the boy remembered was the blinding light from the eyes of the monster that would extinguish his young life.

There was a sickening thud as the boy was violently catapulted into the air like he had been shot from a cannon. But there was no safety net and blood spattered everywhere as his head hit the tree stump. Neighbors came running out to help, but there was nothing they could do except listen to the hoot owl up in the tree.

* * *

Sometimes after supper, we would walk up the street by the old Hegeler mansions; a place Alfred Hitchcock would love. In the backyard of the Matthiessen-Hegeler zinc factory, were some really cute goats just waiting to have a little girl pet them. Grandma said the Grandpa at the mansion liked to drink goat's milk. *Yuck! Why would anybody drink goat's milk? And how exactly do you milk a goat?* Grandma only laughed. "You sure do ask a lot of questions, don't you?" she said. "Why don't we just go up there and feed them?"

On the way, we had to pass the backyard of one of the mansions. It was surrounded by a tall iron fence. Since the residence was no longer occupied, the grounds had become overgrown with small trees and thick underbrush giving the place a real eerie feeling much like in the movies. But that didn't stop this curious little girl.

I pressed my face as close as possible against the tall fence. Staring intently, my eyes scanned the premises. Deep within the tangled grounds I spotted a child's swing set with two swings. *Wow, that's nice. Wonder who it belongs to.*

"It belongs to me!"

Frozen in my tracks I found myself face-to-face with a little girl. She was about six years old, but her clothes were not like mine. Instead she was wearing a dress with a high collar, black stockings, black laced shoes and a big white bow in her hair.

She reached her hand through the fence and touched my arm. Her fingers felt cold even though it was summer. "Come play with me," she said. "We have two swings."

There weren't any little girls on my block to play with and the invitation seemed inviting. However, remembering my encounter with the mysterious boy at the farm, I was hesitant to join her even though we were from the same neighborhood. Something about this wasn't right and I quickly pulled my arm away. *I can't play now. We're going to go see the goats. Are those your animals?*

"Please," she pleaded. "It will be ok."

Although fighting the temptation to go with her, I cried *No!* With a sad look on her face, I watched as she turned and walked through the little trees; right THROUGH the actual trees and disappeared! I looked over my shoulder for Grandma and ran to catch up with her wondering if I should tell her about my new friend.

***

As I grew older, many unexplainable events unfolded. As soon as the lights were out at bedtime, strange visitors bearing unusual messages would come calling. Who they were would be anybody's guess. I wasn't interested in knowing. I just wanted them to go away and leave me alone. But no, they insisted on hovering over my bed or sometimes getting right up in my face where I would get a good look at their haunting eyes.

One night, all I saw was a hand coming toward my face. Quickly I sought refuge under the covers. When I finally mustered enough courage to take a peek, it was gone; hopefully gone back through that mysterious door or passage way that had been opened. I was certain it had not been me that let them in. That song kept playing in my mind: There's someone in my head, but it's not me." Even though these people were strangers to me, they all seemed to know my name. How could that be possible? Where had we met before? Grandma once told me about fairies, but I was certain these visitors came from another place.

I pulled the covers over my head a lot. My heart would beat so fast I feared it would burst. I would scream and wake everybody up. My mother took me to the doctor and told him about my episodes. I attempted to explain the strange happenings to him. After all, he was a doctor. Surely I could trust him to understand. But of course, he didn't believe any part of my story. Instead he looked me right in the eye as he concluded I was a little girl with an overactive imagination that didn't want to go to bed at night. *Really?* Maybe I could imagine diverting the visitors over to his house some night when they decided to manifest. Perhaps then we could have another go at that conversation.

After that, whenever I felt something wicked coming my way, I would hug my teddy bear real tight and think *Go away!* That usually worked. One thing was for sure, I always slept in the middle of the bed. That way there was no chance of anybody grabbing my hand during the night. Just because somebody tells you there isn't anything under your bed doesn't make it so.

Soon I found myself having the most unbelievable and lucid dreams. Many times I felt myself flying high over the countryside much like a super hero. Was I really dreaming or was I having an out-of-body experience? After waking up, I could remember everything down to the minute detail including sounds and smells. And these dreams were in living color. Oh yes, nothing but the best for me. Red was the dominant color. There would always be something red in my dream. Days or maybe weeks later, events in my life would unfold exactly as they appeared in the dream. It was as if I were watching a movie for the second time. It was scary, interesting and mind blowing all at the same time.

I knew when visitors were coming before they drove up in their car. The phone didn't get a chance to ring without me picking up the receiver and connecting with the caller first. It was all becoming, excuse the pun, spooky. I wasn't sure what I was or how this special gift was bestowed upon me, but I was starting to appreciate its value and wasn't giving it back.

Could it have been inherited from Grandma? As I recall, there were similar peculiarities surrounding her. Whenever somebody was going to have a baby, she would dangle a needle and thread over their stomach. When asked if it was a boy or girl, the needle would sway and give an answer. She was always right. She would speak about listening to the hoot owl predicting ominous events before they occurred. Sometimes she would answer my questions before the words left my lips. It was as though she could hear my thoughts. And actually, there were times I imagined I could hear hers too. Yes, we appeared to be embarked on the same mysterious journey, but why? And where was it leading us?

Exactly how did this special gift work? Why were we selected to be the lucky recipients? I needed answers, but they were not forthcoming. Then one spring day, Grandma quietly slipped into the afterlife taking our secrets with her. How would I ever be able to figure all this out on my own? Perhaps I was just crazy after all. But the voices in my head said, "No!"

So was I different? Sometimes I wondered. While other girls were worrying about what to wear Saturday night or wondering if that cute guy might ask them out, I found my solace being deeply immersed in the caverns of the unknown. Many a night, like Edgar Allen Poe wrote, "I pondered weak and weary" over the plethora of wonders surrounding me. Why was Stonehenge built so as to align with the sun marking the Summer and Winter Solstices? What was the purpose of creating the ancient Nazca Lines in Peru? Who was this race of giants found buried in mounds? Or how was I able to stand at the foot of my bed and look at myself lying there? There were so many things I couldn't explain and so many extenuating circumstances beyond my control.

My affinity for seeking answers brought me to read every article and book pertaining to these subjects that I could get my hands on. My fascination or perhaps obsession with all things mysterious and strange grew by leaps and bounds. Like a ravenous carnivore, I simply devoured this delectable food for thought.

And yet, all the while a continuous on flex of whispers from beyond the grave took refuge inside my head. For a time I attempted to turn it off until that moment when I would be able to fully comprehend it all. Of course, now I know that wasn't an option; you can only turn down the volume. So as the wandering souls searching for salvation reached out to me, I made myself available to lend a sympathetic ear.

It took me years to process before I came to realize my true potential; I was in possession of an uncanny ability to communicate with the afterlife. Even though I was able to see, hear and feel spirit, never in my wildest imagination did it occur to me that I could have an ongoing exchange of words on an intellectual level with one. That was until the day my Great Grandmother Elizabeth, whom I had never met, whispered, "Hello, it's me!"

Hegeler mansion LaSalle, IL

Giants at Dickson Mounds, Lewistown, IL

Grandma's photos

"Hello darkness, my old friend,
 I've come to talk with you again,
 Because a vision softly creeping,
 Left its seeds while I was sleeping
 And the vision that was planted in my brain
 Still remains within the sounds of silence."

--- Simon & Garfunkel

Chapter 2

Hello, It's Me

After endorsing the backs of the checks, I hurriedly entered the information on my deposit slip. There were numerous items on my to-do-list starting with the bank. Then I looked down and saw I had inadvertently written 8-29 as the date. *Why the heck did you do that? It's only June. You know the hurrier you go the behinder you get.* I grabbed another slip and filled it out. Much to my dismay, I had again written 8-29. What was wrong with me? Why was I doing this?

My hand reached for another slip. Realizing this was the last one, it had better be correct. This time I concentrated on what I was doing and did it correctly. I took a deep breath and decided to sit there a few minutes and collect my thoughts. *How in the world did you get so mixed up? Tell me this isn't an indication of how the rest of the day is going to progress or not.*

I picked up the pen and paper and attempted to compile a shopping list. It was probably fruitless because at the rate it was going, I would leave it behind on the table. It doesn't make much sense. How could a person with abilities, do such a thing? It wasn't very logical if you asked me.

Suddenly, an invisible yet forceful hand grabbed my wrist and set it down upon the paper. I could feel each finger as it wrapped firmly around my wrist. I had heard of automatic writing, but never experienced it. A stern voice called out, "I said 8-29!" At that moment, an eerie feeling came over me. Some unseen force took control of my hand as I was compelled to write their message. The pen seemed to have a mind of its own as it scrolled 8-29 over and over again.

But as quickly as the mysterious hand fought for control over mine, it relinquished its grasp. Obviously, somebody was quite content that their message had been delivered. I suppose since I wasn't paying attention when they were trying to get through, they lent me a helping hand so to speak. But what did it mean? Better yet, who was this strange visitor and where did they go in such a hurry? I sat quietly for a few minutes awaiting further instructions, but none came.

After completing my various tasks and yes, having remembered the shopping list, I returned home. I was quite pleased with myself to have found a great deal on candles. Lately, lighting a candle had become part of my daily routine. I found the flickering light both relaxing and entertaining. I always noticed the flame had a peaceful glow. Sometimes it seemed to sway back and forth doing a happy dance. Other times it would jump up and down with great enthusiasm. Many spiritual workers have the belief that the candle flame can actually pierce the veil between our own physical world and the spiritual world. This can create a passageway or portal that allows communication to exist.

Today the flame was unusually feisty. Immediately after the match made contact with the wick, it sparked a flame that seemed to have a mind of its own. It began to slowly rise up and down and for awhile, it twisted and turned. Then it started to jump except it was leaping a lot higher than usual. The center became bright red and almost resembled a glowing eye; one that was watching me.

It was a bit frightening to watch, but on the other hand, it appeared to command my attention. Suddenly, the flame that was obviously guided by some hidden power began to rapidly shoot up as much as three inches. Its intention was threatening. *Yikes!* I had never encountered a deranged flame before. What should I do? My first thought was to extinguish it before anything bad happened. But if what they say is true, I didn't want to interrupt the spirits as they were attempting to conquer some sinister energy around me. They seemed to be working with such enthusiasm. I concluded it would be best to just stay back at a safe distance until the battle was over.

After the most sensational light show I had ever witnessed, the flame lowered then faded to black. It had truly been a stupendous performance. The audience applauded. But wait, there was an encore. A quiet voice whispered from stage right, "Look."

For some strange reason I was compelled to reach for the diminished remains of the defeated candle. I found it to be peculiar when after that rousing display of energy, the wax had settled to one side. I picked up the plate to examine it closer. "Look," the voice whispered.

As I began to slowly rotate the plate around, it seemed as though there might be some sort of shape there. My first thought was it looked almost as if a woman was cradling a baby in her arms. How could this be? Perhaps, it was just matrixing. In paranormal studies this is when the brain finds familiar shapes in an image and tells your eyes what to see.

On that note, I rubbed my obviously confused eyes and prepared to take another look. But before I could reassess the situation, I was interrupted. "Hello, it's me. That's right. It's me holding you when you were a baby," the voice whispered. "I was there when you were born and I will always be with you."

Whoa! What just happened? For a moment, I was beside myself and stood there in total disbelief. Or should I say there was something beside myself as I was sure there was a presence at my right side. I could feel their warmth. *Who are you?* I wondered. There was no response. Nervously I turned around, but there was no one there.

Who was this person talking to me? Was it somebody I knew? Was it them who orchestrated that fantastic light show? They said something about being there when I was born. Maybe it's Grandma. My mother lived with her before I was born because my father was in the army. Surely she was there the day I arrived. It would be greatly appreciated to have her around again to help me with all the weirdness in my life.

So mystery solved. My Grandma had come back to be with me once again. I wasn't sure how or why this happened, but it's truly going to be a real pleasure communicating with her. Now I felt better knowing who was whispering to me.

* * *

A few months later, I was driving home and missed my turn. *I hate when that happens. Focus will you?* I hadn't driven very far when up ahead there was a strip mall. Good, now pull in, get turned around and pay attention. As I looked to my left, the sign Gemini Moon caught my eye. It was the metaphysical store my friend Toni had told me about. This was one of her favorite places. She thought I might find it interesting.

I had been promising myself for the longest time to stop by, but never got around to it. Today seemed like a perfect opportunity to visit. There must have been a reason I turned down this street. There are no mistakes they say.

The sign in the window said psychics were available today. It sounded inviting, but I was quite pleased with Toni Sun's messages as she was always spot on. Of course, there's nothing like a second opinion. Who knows? I would have to mill this over in my misguided mind while browsing the store.

A hint of sandalwood incense lingered in the air creating the perfect ambiance. There was an array of renaissance clothing, jewelry and books. Every table featured some kind of beautiful gemstone and crystal. Of course, what else would I have expected to find? Toward the back were herbs, sage and CANDLES! *Oh, my!* This was a very interesting place indeed. I could easily get into trouble here.

I decided to walk back to the candles, go figure. Surely a person can never have too many. That's especially true if, like me, you insist on lighting one every day. I just needed to assure myself there would always be a rainbow of colors within my grasp. It's not like an obsession. I could quit anytime. It's just the Girl Scout in me wanting to be prepared and I'm sticking with that story.

As I made my way over to my temptation, I passed a little room where a man doing a reading. Maybe I would stop and talk to him after shopping. I wasn't sure. It felt rather uncomfortable walking into a place and considering a reading with somebody I had never met before.

My goodness, there were so many candles that it was going to be difficult to make a decision. I found myself in quite a quandary. My eyes got wide and I felt like a kid in a candy store; some deranged kid. *Ok, better calm down before you scare somebody.* Feeling a bit embarrassed, I looked around to see if anyone had been watching me. It appeared I had been spared this time at least.

I was just about to turn back when I overheard a conversation. It was a man saying something about how he hoped the person liked the messages he received for them. I wasn't aware there had been two people reading that day. I had the overwhelming feeling I needed to speak with him. As soon as the woman walked away, I quickly approached him before somebody else grabbed him.

I asked if I might have a reading. He seemed a bit surprised at first. He said he was not working now and had just come into the store to visit. Sheri, the store owner, hearing our conversation quickly attempted to defuse a seemingly awkward and embarrassing moment. She told me the other man was available and was sure I would like him. Why not speak with him? But before I could answer, the man smiled and said it would be ok. He asked if it would be all right to use one of the rooms. She said yes.

He escorted me over to the little room and we sat down. Now that this was actually happening, I was starting to have some second thoughts. *What the heck are you doing? I thought you were going to think about this more? Where is your head today?* But then a voice whispered, "It's ok." Feeling a bit guilty I apologized profusely for intruding on his day off. He told me not to give it a second thought because he felt he was being guided to do this.

He began by telling me his name was Jeffery. He immediately sensed there was a woman standing on my right side. She was the one that brought us together today.

I smiled, nodded and told him it was my Grandma. She was always there. I asked him if he could describe how she looked. He said she looked like me, was slender, had dark hair, but was shorter.

He told me she had a message for me. She whispered, "Don't forget the candle." *Well, that was a very strange message.* I guess I was expecting something more profound. I asked him what that meant, but he didn't know. He told me to think about it a few days and it would most likely make more sense. Perhaps he wasn't hearing correctly since she spoke with an accent. She might have been saying candle sticks.

Accent? My grandma didn't speak with an accent. He said she was indeed speaking with something like a Polish accent. He also felt it wasn't a grandmother. It was somebody from a generation before that. It was probably more like a Great Grandmother. She was from my mother's side of the family. I asked for her name, but he didn't know. He said she told him again, "Remember the candle."

At that moment, I didn't know what to make of all that. But as I thought more about it, it made sense. I remembered the day of that sensational light show and what happened to the candle wax. Was the woman validating this for me and letting me know it was her that whispered to me that day?

Suddenly, a chill rushed through my entire body and I shivered. I just realized today was August 29. *Oh, my gosh, freaking 8-29!* This had been what she was trying to tell me when she grabbed my hand back in June. Now I wondered if I had been purposely made to miss my turn so that she could lead me here. And did she have something to do with getting Jeffery to come here on his day off so we could meet? Oh yes, this was much more than a coincidence.

All the way home those words echoed over and over in my mind: "Remember the candle." It was amazing I never missed a turn this time since the truck was almost operating on automatic pilot. Who was this woman? What did she mean she was there when I was born? How could that be possible? I had so many questions and so few answers. It just wasn't fair. I was more confused than ever.

"History," the voice whispered. *History? What the heck is that supposed to mean? Can you do any better than that?* I guess I was expecting a response, but nothing came. Wait a minute. Was she talking about the family tree? I suppose somebody from a long time ago would refer to it as history. I remember last year I was given papers with some names and dates. Was it there?

I hurried through the door in search of answers. Where did I put those papers? I recall tucking them inside a folder. They didn't seem that important to me at the time. Wow, little did I know what a mistake that would turn out to be. Think; think where did you put them? *Hey, whoever you are, could you help me out here?* But no, now there was only silence.

Where oh where was that family tree folder? I knew it was somewhere in a safe place. It had to be in the desk. But as soon as I opened the drawer, I feared the worst. Over the past year, my stash had grown tremendously. Yes, I had become a folder hoarder. And to make matters worse none of the folders were marked. Note to self: label folders.

As I set the pile on the floor, I let out a deep sigh. Might we as well get comfortable. This was going to be a long tedious process. Upon opening each folder, there was the new found joy that came with discovering yet another item that had been put in a safe place. As the stack began to dwindle, I started to panic. What if it wasn't here? Finally, there was one remaining folder. *Please be in here. I promise to put it within reach from now on.*

My fingers appeared to move in slow motion as they revealed the contents. Inside the folder were three old pieces of paper. How old would be anybody's guess. The pages were yellowed from time. Somebody had attempted to record the family genealogy years ago, the author was unknown. One page was handwritten, but no one recognized the writing. The two other pages were from an old typewriter.

I had looked over this information once before and made a feeble attempt at researching the family history, but gave up and set it aside. Most of the names meant nothing to me. After all, who would I know from the 1800's? Slowly my eyes moved over the pages. Elizabeth. Her name was Elizabeth.

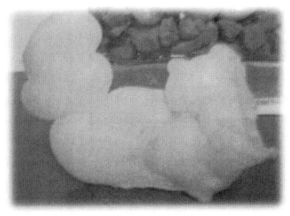

Candle wax that appears to be a woman holding a baby

"No, I won't be afraid
Oh, I won't be afraid
Just as long as you stand,
Stand by me"

--- Ben E. King

Chapter 3

Auras

After some extreme coaxing, a friend finally persuaded me to attend my first yoga class. I recall there being many times when I had pointed out to her that exercise was followed by exorcism in the dictionary. That being said, I had no problem steering away from such ghoulish activities without a second thought.

Once however, I did seriously entertain the idea of jogging. It seemed an easy outlet to get exercise. I imagined myself jogging through the park with my hair blowing in the gentle breeze. The ever watchful sun kept me company as my trust worthy Reeboks guided me along the path. Surely this was the method of least resistance. But then I wondered. Why was it that joggers always seemed to find the dead bodies? Well, something about that thought seemed to ruin the mood. Anyway, I had heard good things about yoga. It was supposed to be relaxing and it seemed harmless enough. Why not? What could it hurt? It was time to explore something new.

I recently spent six fun filled weeks lounging on the couch nursing a fractured foot and torn tendon. One thing was for sure. When I do something, I take pride in myself and shoot for the stars. I had been relating to people the story of how I met my misfortune. I was hang gliding in Telluride, jumped off the mountain and miscalculated the downdraft. Unfortunately, my story was so convincing that no one saw past my sarcasm and I was forced to give it up.

In the beginning, I enjoyed my little sabbatical occasionally drowning my sorrows with doses of Dove chocolates. But soon that portly hunk of plaster had become much like an unwanted guest that had over stayed its welcome. I tried my best to be gracious, but I thought he'd never leave. Not that I wouldn't miss that beautiful creature with all its charm. Mind you, I wore it proudly and professed it to be the newest fashion statement. As I clomped along as gracefully as could be, people stared at me and I knew how much they secretly wanted to be me.

But now, with its departure, all the finer joys of life were possible again. I was looking forward to some uninterrupted sleep. Now I could finally roll over in bed without waking up because that dreadful thing attacked me when I wasn't looking. No more hobbling up and down the stairs hoping the entire time my body would remain in an upright position. And at last I could finally scratch that annoying itch that had been just out of reach.

And best of all, those little feet could now wear matching shoes. Being so elated and not able to contain themselves from celebrating their new found freedom, the little guys were inspired to perform a happy dance. However, this little number didn't make it past curtain call. Although it had good intentions, like Lowell George sang, "The mind makes some promises the body can't keep." Surely, my ankle had not forgotten how to dance? No, in fact, it didn't have the faintest idea it was supposed to even hold me up. Instead, I felt more like a toddler trying to take those first steps. Alas, sadly there would be no dancing for me.

We would be just minding our own business and without warning the old ankle would fold up. I could see where this was going to create a problem. The doctor told me as soon as the cast was removed everything would be good as new. Plainly this was not the case here. Evidently, somebody forgot to inform my ornery extremity. Obviously, it did not get the foot note. It was acting out and expressing a few ideas of its own. Or maybe it wasn't even thinking for that matter. *Hey, you. Vacation is over. It's time for some support.* Well, attending this class might not be such a bad idea after all. Maybe some yoga exercises were just what I needed.

Surprisingly the day of the class, I was actually quite excited anticipating a hopeful outcome. I felt it was going to be a good experience for me. As I entered the room, I counted six of us. That seemed like an intimate class size. As the lights dimmed, the instructor lit some candles. Flute music softly played in the background. The tiny orange flames flickered back and forth as if they were dancing. There was a magical ambiance about it all. Ah, this was going to be so relaxing.

He asked us to find a place and be seated on the floor. I looked around the room to see my fellow participants. They looked like a nice group of ladies. *Hey, except for those two sitting on their own yoga mats and wearing the official yoga attire.* Now I was going to be subjected to the sight of these two beautiful swans gracefully performing the positions. While I on the other hand, would probably be waddling along like the ugly duckling.

The instructor said his name was Boe and he was a Shaman. He started out by explaining the fundamentals of yoga. This 5000 year old Hindu discipline includes breath control and meditation while assuming specific body postures. The word means "union" of the physical body and the spirit. He assured us that his class was easy enough for beginners and we would take it slow. No muscles would be injured on his watch. He asked who had taken classes in the past. Of course, those two women proudly raised their hands. Boo! I breathed a sigh of relief because nobody else did. Hopefully, I would be able to blend in easily with no problem.

The instructor said we would start out with some basic stretching exercises to warm up. That sounded simple enough. I felt it was actually a good idea since I hadn't done a substantial amount of exercising in the past six weeks. Come to think about it, those curls I did while lifting the Tostitos from the salsa to my mouth probably didn't count.

First he demonstrated the Warrior pose because he said we were all warriors. He encouraged us to duplicate it. *Well, so far so good.* He moved around the room as he checked each one of us to ensure we were doing the position properly. He reminded everyone to concentrate on their breathing as we continued along. Yoga was all about breathing. He proceeded to introduce more poses. And we, being the great students that we were, followed along in like fashion. *Hey, I think I'm getting the hang of it.* He was very pleased with us and praised our success.

Now we were going to do another called Downward Dog. Just like before, I studied how gracefully Boe demonstrated the pose. He made everything look so easy. I carefully stretched my legs into position. *Ouch. Hey, didn't I say yoga seemed harmless enough?* My rebellious ankle seemed to think otherwise. Suddenly, there was excruciating pain radiating across my foot. It felt as though lightening had struck me. With that said my ankle tucked itself inward, knocked me to the floor and I performed my own interpretation of Downward Dog; Play Dead. The instructor rushed to my rescue. He picked me up and brushed off my bruised ego. He assured me that I would be able to master this pose providing I moved slowly. *Ok, let's give it another try.* This time everything went well. *Good dog.*

As the class progressed, we slowly evolved like the metamorphosis of caterpillars transforming into beautiful butterflies. Soon we triumphantly discovered our inner greatness thanks to the guidance of our knowledgeable and extremely patient instructor. It also helped that he didn't laugh. Or at least he didn't laugh out loud.

Boe thanked us and applauded everybody on our first performance. He said he was going to reward us with a special surprise by doing an Aura Reading for everybody. The aura is an electromagnetic field that surrounds every living being. This is seen as layers of colors. Everybody's aura is unique.

First off, he wanted to show us something interesting. He said he was glad I came for my ankle would serve as an example. Kneeling down on the floor beside me, he instructed everyone to watch closely. Boe gazed down upon one ankle and explained what color surrounded it. As I concentrated, I could amazingly see what he was talking about. To our surprise, when he moved over to the cantankerous ankle, the color was completely different. He explained it was because the injury had not fully healed yet. That was very impressive. *Ok, little guy, I forgive your awkwardness.*

One by one, we took our place against the wall. He extinguished all but one candle so that the wall was softly illuminated. As each person was seated there with their eyes closed, Boe asked everyone to stare at the wall behind them. After a few moments of looking intently, we might be able to observe the person's aura. Even though none of us had ever done this before, we discovered we had a hidden talent. We could, indeed, see a halo of color surrounding each person. And he was correct about each one of us having a unique color all our own.

Filled with anticipation, I wondered what would be in store for me. *What color would my aura be? What else might he observe about me?* As I lowered myself to the floor, as if on cue, my ankle played a dirty trick on me and kindly tucked itself inward once more. I swear I heard it laughing as I lost my balance and almost fell over. *Nice move, Grace. There's nothing like ruining the moment.*

I closed my eyes and tried to be as Boe would say, "one with the universe." He said he was beginning to see colors surrounding me. There was also a glowing light by my side. At that moment, I could feel the presence of Elizabeth on my right. *You know what would be fun? Why don't you let him see you?* A few seconds later, with excitement in his voice, he said he could see somebody by my side. *Thank you, Elizabeth.*

Suddenly, I felt her enter my body. I could feel the warm vibrations she was emitting. I was quite taken aback as she had never done that before, but of course, I did ask her to show herself. I wasn't sure what to expect, but I put my trust in her.

Boe looked at me and exclaimed, "Something is happening to your face! What is going on?" It was morphing right before his eyes. Then any resemblance of my face had vanished. In its place was the face of my great grandmother. I ever so slightly opened my eyes and glanced around the room being careful not to move my head; or was it her head? Everyone appeared to be mesmerized and spellbound over what was happening.

He began to describe her and he was spot on. He started to communicate with her and remarked about feeling her warm presence. She showed him her favorite cookie jar. He said she liked to cook, but she corrected him. No, she liked to bake.

Soon, I felt her leave my body and go back to my side. He told me she was gone and he could see my face once more. But then, she decided to jump back in. Boe said he could see her face again. As soon as he made that comment, she was gone like a flash. Suddenly, I felt her leap in and out of me several times. This sure gave a new meaning to throwing your weight around. My body was tingling from all the energy. My head was reeling as it was being jerked about from all the action. He said he could see my face continue to change back and forth. He remarked that he had never seen anything such as this before.

Suddenly, I heard her laugh, "Ha ha, I'll bet!" She was having such a great time toying with him. Finally, after having her way with him, she decided she had had enough fun. She left my body and stood quietly beside me. Boe said he was totally exhausted after that reading. You would have thought Elizabeth would have been tired too. After all, it must have taken a tremendous amount of energy to have performed that feat. But evidently she had been using my energy because I felt drained as well. Who knew yoga could be such an enlightening experience.

"You're my angel.
  Come and save me tonight.
  You're my angel.
  Come and make it all right"

--- Aerosmith

Chapter 4

Rescuing Rosco

It was Tuesday morning and once again I found a new project commanding my attention; the picture frame layout. My goodness this was going to be an exciting undertaking. No, not really. I was being facetious. But seriously, what could possibly be exciting about all these rectangles and squares? The way I look at it, until you've placed a photo inside, if you've seen one frame, you've seen them all.

I let out a sigh and attempted to get myself motivated. Looking over the printout, the task seemed simple enough. It appeared so easy that I was certain I could knock it out in no time. *So let's get started already.*

Clearing everything off the shelves was half the battle. Wondering where to lay it on the floor until you needed it was another problem. *How in the world did all this fit on the shelf?* Looking at the frames all lined up, they reminded me of the squares on the opening of the Brady Bunch where all the kids were looking at each other. Oh no, now I had that song in my head! What would Marcia do? My guess is she would just finish this as quickly as possible and not prolong the agony.

As I began placing each of the frames into their new location, a profound thought entered my mind. *Where did they find these people with the cheesy smiles that posed for the packaging photos? And what were they smiling about?* Perhaps they were thinking, "Sure sucks to be you right now."

And suck it did because it never fails that when you've got merchandise all over the floor everybody needs to walk down that aisle. *Really?* Soon I was starting to feel like the little hamster running on the wheel. Even though I was moving fast, I was not getting anywhere. This project was taking forever and I still had that song in my head, "That's the way we became the Brady Bunch."

As my motions became almost mechanical, I found myself totally oblivious of the world around me. Then the connotation about a picture being worth a thousand words crossed my mind. Suddenly out of the blue, I caught what sounded like a voice behind me. I'm not sure how high I jumped. "You need to stop by the Animal Welfare Society on the way home and look at dogs," they whispered. *Wow, did not expect anyone to take me literally.*

All of a sudden I felt a tug at my heart strings and rightfully so for it had only been three days since Dakota, my beloved lab, suddenly took that journey over the rainbow bridge. The dude, as he liked to be called, was only eight years young. The angels had lured him away from this world much too soon. For heaven's sake, there were countless walks left to take and all those squirrels to chase. He was my best friend, faithful companion and beyond a doubt irreplaceable. How in the world could I even consider thinking about another dog so soon? That was a crazy notion. Where did that come from anyway? I tried to put the thought out of my mind and attempted to focus my attention on what I was doing. Work seemed to provide some distraction for me.

But as my fingers touched a particular frame, one with paw prints, a voice said, "Isn't this nice? He will look so cute in this one. We should get it." *Ok, that's enough already. Some people have things to do here.*

But, oh no, there it was again. That voice said, "You really need to stop by Animal Welfare tonight." I shook my head and wondered why I was thinking this?

Maybe my energy levels were being depleted and I was getting delirious. Or perhaps it was because the building was right down the street from home and I looked at it every day as I drove by. It must have riveted itself deep into my mind like a subliminal message. That's all it was. Maybe I would go there someday, but not any time in the foreseeable future. Right now, I needed to stay on track with my project and not think about it anymore. I was so close to finishing.

As I stepped into the parking lot at the end of the day, I was in a state of euphoria having conquered that layout and best of all those voices. I slid the key into the ignition, tuned the radio to WRIF and started to drive home. "You're my angel. Come and save me tonight," the song said. Even though I had heard that song many times before, this time it was as if somebody was singing it especially for me.

As I merged onto the highway, a voice said, "Just stop by and take a look. What's it going to hurt? It's right on your way home." *Oh, my gosh. Make it stop already!* I was sure someday I would go over there and look at the dogs. There were probably several I might like, but it was just too soon.

I turned the volume up in an attempt to drown out any other sounds. Unfortunately, that did not work. The voice pleaded, "Please listen to the song." I complied and "You're the reason I live," came through the speakers.

Ok, I give up. I couldn't seem to get the thought out of my head. *Maybe I will stop on the way home. Are you satisfied?* Of course, I knew I wouldn't.

I drove the rest of the way in silence. By that I mean there were no more comments from that voice. I got off the highway and headed down the street toward my house. Up ahead, was the Animal Welfare Society. For just a split second I actually had an inkling about going, but decided it was just not right. Maybe I would go in another month. Or so I thought.

"You have to go." The voice was back. "You have to go today!" they insisted. I thought about it for a moment and decided I would go tomorrow. They probably weren't even open. And as if somebody was reading my mind, they responded, "They most certainly are open and he won't be there tomorrow!" they yelled.

Ok, all right already, I guess I'm going to go look at dogs. Did you say he? Is there a particular dog I'm supposed to find? Now I was getting sarcastic. I wasn't expecting an answer, but there it was. "He's in the cage by the front desk. He's a little red dog and his name is Rosco. He won't be there tomorrow. You have to go now!" *All right!*

On that note, I looked for the driveway and slowly turned into the parking lot. Sure enough, they were still open. I got out and half heartedly started walking to the door not quite sure what I was doing there or what to expect.

As I entered the lobby, there was a lot going on considering how late in the day it was. There were still several people waiting at the desk. Two women were near the window dangling some string as they played with a tabby cat. A couple sat on the chairs by the entrance holding the cutest little black lab puppy. He reminded me so much of Dakota. I sat down next to them and watched while they rubbed his little ears. He looked up with his big brown eyes and gave them lots of puppy kisses. *What the heck were you thinking? This is so wrong for so many reasons. Let's just slither our way out of here before anybody sees you.*

I looked away for a minute and checked the front desk. They were so busy they most likely never saw me arrive. If I were going to make my escape, I had better get packing. There was no reason I couldn't come back another day.

But as I turned, low and behold, there was indeed a cage by the wall across from the desk. Inside was a small golden retriever dog. He was lying down peacefully and just taking it all in. Within an instant, our eyes met. He had the most beautiful brown eyes. He jumped up, wagged his tail and tried to get my attention. It was as if he were calling out to me, beckoning me to come over. I tried to resist, but his gaze was bewitching and overpowering.

The woman at the desk looked up and asked if she could help me. *Oh no, too late.* There was no chance of sneaking out now. Slowly, feeling like I was in a trance, I walked toward her. I still wasn't sure what I was doing there. Suddenly, I found myself telling her I thought I would like to see the dog in the cage. My head felt strange. It was almost as if I were under his spell. She told me there were many more dogs in back. Would I like to come with her and look around? She would be glad to take me there.

I glanced back at the couple sitting in the chairs. The little puppy was so cute. It really reminded me of Dakota. Oh, I missed him so much. How I wished I could hug him more time and rub my nose in his soft fur. How could I ever snuggle with somebody else?

But then I looked over at those sad little eyes staring at me from the cage. Perhaps for a moment, he thought I was walking away like all the others. But walking didn't appear to be an option for me since my legs seemed to be frozen in place. Yes, I was under his spell. Without a doubt, I needed to see this one.

Finally, my legs regained some feeling. We walked over to the cage. As soon as she opened the door, he started whining and was all over me. He was so soft and fluffy. "This is the one," the voice said. "Dakota and I picked him out for you. Sweetheart, say 'hi' to your new mommy." As if responding to the voice, he winked at me and gave me a big wet kiss. I couldn't believe it, but for some reason it felt so good.

The woman told me I had been fortunate in coming by tonight. They only keep animals there for a few months. Then they send them to another location in hopes that they will get more exposure and be adopted. He had been there for quite a while. Most people want to adopt puppies. He was a year and a half. She said he was a very gentle boy. His owners had purchased a new house and didn't want a dog there. *My goodness, that's so sad!* They were going to send him away in the morning. It was a good thing I had found him tonight.

Then she asked me if I wanted to know his name. I couldn't believe my ears as she said it was Rosco. *Well, of course, it was.* Again, I got a shiver all over my body. This was utterly insane. But yet on the other hand, it felt so very right. If Dakota wants me to take this dog home, then let's do it. I looked at the woman and asked where I could sign the adoption papers. She seemed a bit surprised about my quick decision. Little did she know, I had been thinking about this all day so, of course, it was time to rescue my Rosco and bring him home.

Rosco

"Would you know my name,
If I saw you in heaven?
Would it be the same,
If I saw you in heaven?"

--- Eric Clapton

Chapter 5

Dakota

Even after welcoming my little buddy Rosco into my home with hopes of filling the emptiness, it simply did not feel complete without my Dakota. My big boy was much more than a dog to me; he was my best friend. Throughout the nine short years we were together, we shared many precious and unforgettable moments.

Beneath that soft black Labrador fur, beat an incredible heart filled with unconditional love. Happiness exuded from his cold nose to the tip of his waggy tail. And he never ceased to amaze me as he showered me with endless kisses. Wise beyond his years, he taught me life's little secrets including the joy of sharing; the couch, the bed and my food. It was all good.

My devoted companion was constantly by my side following me everywhere and keeping a watchful eye out for me. And strangely enough, I know we were able to communicate telepathically. "Are you going to eat all that? … I love you, mommy!" We were together so much that sometimes I didn't know where my shadow ended and his began. Yes, we were almost inseparable.

One day I discovered a website with some really cool dog toys. Each toy had a mechanism that emitted the life-like sound of that particular animal. The page had a button enabling you to listen to each one before ordering. My dude and I would sit in front of the computer as I clicked on each animal. I asked him which ones he liked and he would wag his tail approving of the selection. No, there was nothing at all odd about me.

He was a rambunctious ball of energy as he raced around the living room squeezing each one of his animals and flinging them up into the air. It sounded like a day at the zoo especially when he continuously squeezed the poor monkey. After the adrenaline rush had subsided, he would find his baby hedge hog and snuggle next to me on the couch; a heartbeat at my feet.

When we were watching the weather forecast, he would always think they were talking about him when they mentioned South Dakota. His favorite TV program was Law and Order, the original one, of course. He would get up close to the screen and listen for the theme song. "Boom, boom." His tail would wag. When the clarinet part came, his ears quivered. If the show started and he wasn't in the room, rest assured, he would come leaping down the hallway to listen to his favorite song.

Like his mommy, he also enjoyed watching paranormal shows. I remember the night on Ghost Hunters when Brian yelled, "Dude, run!" Dakota tilted his head back and with a grin from ear to ear made a sound like, "Ha, ha! He looked back at me with those big brown eyes to see if I agreed. Without a doubt, he was laughing. And he was absolutely right. It was priceless.

When Zak on Ghost Adventures would say, "And this is why we are here," Dakota would laugh and nod his head. Giving the expression watch dog a new meaning, he would sit quietly and study each episode as if he was reviewing evidence. Occasionally, I would notice him fixating on something before running up to the screen to get a closer look. I really do believe at times he was actually following along with the investigation. Sometimes I swore he saw or heard things I missed.

I would often call him my hero because he always helped me find the laughter in every situation. But now that he had journeyed over the rainbow bridge, there didn't seem to be much to smile about any more. Even though he was gone, he had forever left paw prints on my heart. Hopefully, this little Rosco he picked out for me would help me smile again. Only time would tell.

It seemed Rosco was a rather quiet boy. He wasn't the excitable guy I had first met. I had a new name picked out for him, but he just looked like a Rosco to me. I knew it must have been scary for him being in yet another strange place. But we would have to take care of that. Perhaps if I tossed around a few toys with him, he would feel more at ease. I never did gather up Dakota's toys. They were still sitting in the corner of the room.

I reached over and picked up the frog. This had been one of Dakota's favorites. Surely he would like it too. However, when I threw it to him, he ducked and it ended up down the hallway. *Come on, Rosco. Let's play.* I grabbed the koala and squeezed it. But when it giggled, he got scared and hopped up onto the loveseat instead. *What's the matter? Why won't you play with me?*

He just gave me a puzzled look, glanced down the hallway and rested his little head down on his paws. *Ok, then why don't you come over here and sit by me?* He didn't seem to pay any attention to me at all. Obviously, he had no interest in interacting with me one way or another. *What's the matter, Rosco? Mommy is very sad and needs somebody to play with her.* He looked at me as if to say, "Sounds like a personal problem." Then he let out a disgusted sigh and closed his eyes.

Having felt defeated, I decided to watch TV. As I picked up the remote, I looked over at him one more time. *I sure wish somebody would play with me, but I guess not.* Just as I was about to turn the TV on, I heard, "Rib bit, rib bit, rib bit," coming from down the hall. Thinking he had changed his mind, I looked up. But he was still on the loveseat. He looked at me as if to say, "It wasn't me."

Was that you, Dakota? Did you squeeze the frog for mommy? Oh, that's crazy. Of course, that didn't happen. You imagined the whole thing. Then I heard it again, "Rib bit, rib bit, rib bit." Had my Dakota come back to visit me? You bet. Suddenly, I felt like I was standing in a rainbow. I now had the best of both worlds; Rosco and my angel dog Dakota.

Soon I began experiencing all sorts of unusual things. One night as we were on the couches watching TV, there was a cool draft on my left side. Right after that, I could feel Dakota licking my fingers. His fur brushed up against my arm. Out of the corner of my eye I saw him walk past the TV and head down the hallway. *Hey, Dude, are you going to sleep without me?* It soon became a nightly event as he continued his usual bedtime routine. I know Rosco would see him too. At first, the little guy seemed befuddled. After all, wasn't he the only dog in this house? *It's ok, Rosco. That's Dakota. He's our friend.* I suppose in the beginning it was very perplexing for him watching this shadowy dog walking around and then disappearing. But after awhile, he relaxed and grew accustomed to his ghostly big brother.

A few months later, I was attending a Native Pipe Ceremony at Gemini Moon. Before we began, Bumper, who was leading the ceremony, explained the meaning of the Native custom to us. This was a sacred ritual for connecting the physical and spiritual worlds. The pipe was the link between the earth and the sky. As we smoke, the pipe represents our prayers and the smoke becomes our words.

He directed us to form a circle and take a seat on the floor. As we sat down, the lights were dimmed and flute music played softly in the background. I remember thinking how much Dakota loved the flute. *Wish you were here, Dude*. He asked that we did not speak during the ceremony for we would be creating a relationship with the energy of the universe and the Creator. That bond made between earthly and spiritual realms should not be broken. He would call out to all our ancestors and guides. Afterward, we would feel deeply connected and peaceful.

He began to fill the pipe with tobacco. Tobacco is used to connect the two worlds because the roots of the plant grow deep into the earth and its smoke rises high up into the heavens. The fire in the pipe represents the fire in the sun. The smoke symbolizes the truth being spoken.

After lighting the pipe, he had us stand. As we faced each one, he called out to the four directions, "We call to the West with its life giving rains and spirit world, to the North with strength and honesty, to the East where the sun rises and brings us knowledge and to the South that brings us bounty, medicine and growth." We sat back down on the floor and took our place in the circle once more. He took a puff of the pipe, turned to his left and passed it on to me. We continued to pass the pipe around the circle until the offering was fulfilled.

As we relinquished our worries and entered into a state of tranquility, I could feel the radiant energy encompassing the room. I closed my eyes and opened my psyche to the universe. Slowly the room began to morph as if a portal were opening. Would I make a connection with the spirit realm? Would I meet my ancestors and spirit guides?

A very tall Native man, perhaps better described as a giant for he was almost seven feet tall, appeared to me. He had finely chiseled features and wore his dark hair in one long braid. On his head, a single feather was attached to a thin rawhide band. There was a wider band around his right tricep. He stood on the edge of the river bank near a grove of trees. In his hand he held a mighty bow in anticipation of claiming one of the beavers who had built the nearby dam.

"Remember the way of the beaver," he said. *Oh, my goodness that was such a profound message.* So profound, in fact that I wasn't sure what it meant. *Please help me understand what you are trying to tell me. Oh, and please tell me your name.* "Stands Looking," was all he said and then he was gone.

But before I had the opportunity to fully grasp the meaning of his message I began to feel a cool spot on my left side. The hair on my arms was standing up. *Who is coming through this time?* I got a gentle nudge and it felt as though fur was brushing up against my arm. I looked over and saw Dakota. We were, after all, playing flute music. *Dude, you came!* Sprouting a big doggy grin, he walked back and forth between me and the woman on my left. As he wagged his tail, I could feel the breeze. After he was done dancing, he returned to my side, to lie down between us and started licking my fingers. *Good boy!*

I wondered if anyone else noticed him. I glanced around the circle expecting to catch a reaction from somebody, but couldn't tell. Perhaps I was the only one he was showing himself to.

I looked up and was surprised to see a skunk sitting in the center of the circle. *Really?* He lifted his little head up and looked around the room. *Hey, we're all friends here. Don't spray us!* A few seconds later, he scampered over to Sheri and sat down beside her. *Awe, now she's got a friend too.*

At the conclusion of the ceremony, we all began sharing our experiences. I wasn't going to speak about what had happened. Besides who would believe me? *Hey did you guys see my dancing dog? Hope you didn't mind him joining us.* But being caught up in the moment, I did, however, mention the appearance of the cute little skunk. When I did so, an uncomfortable hush fell over the room. *Ok, now you've done it. Everyone thinks you're crazy. Please somebody else say something.*

I took a deep breath and nervously waited for some kind of reaction. After what seemed like an eternity, but in reality was only a few seconds, Sheri came to my rescue, "Yes, I saw him, too. He was walking around the circle and sat down next to me just like you said. He's my Animal Guide and visits me often." *Whew, thanks for saving me.*

And much to my amazement, the woman next to me said, "You probably won't believe this, but I think there was a dog here. I could feel his tail wag and he was licking my fingers. Then he sat down between us right here." Somebody on the other side of the room said, "Ya, I saw a black dog, too. Oh, that must be one of your animal guides. Is he around often?"

Yes, I'm proud to say that's my Dakota and he's always around!

From time to time I still attend various Native gatherings such as Pipe ceremonies, Pow Wows, and

Grandmother Moon ceremonies. Rest assured, Dakota and Stands Looking will always make an appearance. It's a great feeling knowing they are watching out for me.

Dakota

"The waiting is the hardest part.
Every day you see one more card.
You take it on faith; you take it to the heart.
The waiting is the hardest part."

--- Tom Petty

Chapter 6

Troy Grove

I slipped off my shoes and settled down into my favorite chair. My toes being ever so grateful for being set free playfully scrunched the carpet. Ah, it felt so good. As I sipped my Coke, my eyes wandered toward the window and caught a glimpse of the last moments of a beautiful red sunset. The flickering flame of the candle kept me company as darkness was slowly creeping in.

It had been a bizarre day. While performing my routine nursing duties, I happened upon an extraordinary circumstance. There was an elderly lady who according to her vitals was nearing the end. Unfortunately, as an

Empath I had been deemed with an ominous ability; I can sense death approaching. This apocalyptic power induces a dark feeling of impending doom. Why would a person want this grim ability?

Nevertheless, it was time to go check her vitals. Upon entering the room, I froze in my tracks as I couldn't believe my eyes. Next to the bed was a beautiful winged angel surrounded by a bright light. Undoubtedly, the Angel of Death had come calling. Her presence was warm and loving. My lady's pulse was weak as she held on to the last moments of life. *It's time, isn't it?* The angel looked at me and as she bowed her head, a lone teardrop trickled down her face. I nodded and quietly left the room allowing them some time alone. A few hours later she peacefully transitioned to the other side.

After that experience, I was mentally spent, feeling weary and not able to get myself motivated. And with the little doggie foot warmer I had going on, there was no chance of me moving any time soon. Perhaps I would distract myself with some computer games. I found there was no better remedy to help stimulate the mind than a good word game. Hopefully my Scrabble partners Joan and Veronica would be online. I checked the time and realized it was getting late in the United Kingdom. I had to remember there was a five hour difference.

I was trying to determine my next word when, out of the blue, the word Troy Grove popped into my head.

Well, that wasn't going to work. I didn't even have any of those letters. Carefully I rearranged my letters and strategically placed them on the board forming a 36 point word. *Good job!*

Why would I be thinking about Troy Grove? Did I know somebody there? I had not been to that town since I was a little girl. Grandma and I used to visit some of her friends, but I'm sure they were long gone by now. I didn't remember having any relatives there. This was so very odd.

The place did not have much significance. Its only claim to fame was being the birth place of James Butler "Wild Bill" Hickok, the famous frontier scout. Aside from that, there's not much to talk about. It's just a small town over the bridge from where I used to live. Yet I got the nagging feeling there was something amiss. For some reason I needed to go there. But why in the world would I do that? My gosh, it's five hours away.

The feeling began to get over powering. "Troy Grove, Troy Grove", it started to play over and over in my mind. It was almost like a chant. The only problem was I had no idea who was coming through. Now how in the world would a person be able to concentrate on their next word when they were getting inundated with coded messages?

Surely my sister and I could brain storm and figure this out. How difficult could it be? I looked to see if she was online. Perhaps we could decipher this riddle. There had to be a simple explanation.

I asked her if we had any relatives living in Troy Grove. But then a stranger thought crossed my mind. I wasn't so sure they were living. She told me she wasn't aware of anyone. Why did I ask? I explained how for some reason it popped into my head and no matter how hard I tried, it wouldn't go away. There seemed to be some connection with this place. I was certain there was a relative there. I was just as sure there was a pressing matter I needed to attend to for this person. It just didn't make sense why they had chosen me instead of somebody closer.

* * *

A few days later, I sat down at the computer. No sooner had I begun to type when a strange feeling came over me. Suddenly, there it was again, "Troy Grove." Why on earth was this happening? What was it about this place? The answer was clear as mud. However, somewhere within all the murkiness, I understood far too well how imperative it was for me to go there. Something was irrefutably wrong and I suspected I was the only one that could solve the mystery.

Now how absurd was that? What could possibly be happening that was of such significance? Better yet, why would I be the only person that could be of assistance? After all, I was hundreds of miles away. *Hey, is there somebody slightly closer, maybe in the same state? Oh ya, that's right. I'm probably the only one that can hear you. Lucky me.*

Try as I might, there was no way of getting this thought out of my mind. The more I attempted to divert my attention elsewhere, the louder and more insistent the voice became, "Troy Grove." Who was this mysterious person needing my help? Exactly what was the dilemma commanding my attention? Obviously, it must be of monumental importance since I was becoming obsessed with the very thought and unable to focus on anything else. I found myself in quite a quandary attempting to grasp the gravity of the situation.

* * *

As weeks quickly faded into months, I found I was unable to elude that lingering thought buried deep within the echoes of my mind. Whenever I least expected, there it was that all too familiar rendition, "Troy Grove." It was relentless. The madding part being there was never anything more. It was so frustrating let alone perplexing.

Please, could I persuade somebody to disclose another clue? Could you entrust me with a little more information? Who is there? What do they need? At least point me in the right direction. I waited for an answer. After a long silence, I was about to give up. Then I heard Elizabeth whisper, "You have to go there."

But why? What do you know about all this? Are you insinuating that you're privy to some precious pieces to this puzzle? If so, please enlighten me. I would be traveling to another state, remember? It's not like I could drop everything and leave town. I patiently waited for a reply, but got none. A few minutes later, like a bad penny, it was back, "Troy Grove."

As I was driving to an appointment the next day, I couldn't help but notice what a beautiful spring day it had turned out to be. Finally, it appeared old man winter had retreated and taken away his shades of gray. The sky was blue except for the occasional wisps of cirrus clouds that Mother Nature had strategically placed about. The trees were budding, the blades of grass had perked up again and the air felt so refreshing.

Just then, my eyes wandered over to the cemetery I was passing. Lovely bouquets of flowers dotted the graveyard. The majority of them were yellow daffodils. I was thinking how beautiful the place looked decorated in this sunshine theme.

Suddenly, I heard, "I want yellow flowers on my grave." Needless to say, I was a bit startled. I wasn't expecting this. It was not the sort of surprise you wanted to spring up on you while driving. "Nobody ever puts flowers on my grave," she continued.

Ok, Elizabeth, I promise I'll put some yellow flowers on your grave. The only problem is I'm not sure where that might be. Could you tell me? I waited for a reply, but none came. I continued down the road to my appointment. Perhaps there would be an answer forth coming. I drove the remainder of the way listening intently for a response, but got only silence.

On the way home, wondering if maybe I should take another route, I reluctantly approached the cemetery. Would the sight of those pretty arrangements spark another conversation? Sure enough from over my shoulder, I heard, "I want yellow flowers TOO but my grave is lost!" The voice was almost frantic. It was also unduly loud. I swore the person was sitting next to me, but yet I saw nothing. "Please, you have to find my grave!" she pleaded. Well, I sure wasn't expecting all this conversation about flowers today. I waited and listened, but after the sudden outburst, there was nothing more.

I returned home and saw my sister was online. I mentioned how Elizabeth told me she wanted yellow flowers on her grave. She was very distressed about her grave being lost. Cathy, who is a florist, agreed we should get a bouquet of daffodils from her store and take it to her.

Neither of us was confident about where that might be. As a child I remembered taking trips to St. Vincent's cemetery. There were four white wooden crosses standing in a row. It was too long ago for me to recall the names. Even if I did, as I took a mental picture of the place, the crosses only had first names on them. Of course, even finding her first name on one of them would be a step in the right direction. Then we could get those flowers on her grave like she wanted. Hopefully, it would help her feel better.

We began to brain storm and analyze what few clues we had. Surely I could get a few more hints from Elizabeth. My sister would take a ride to the cemetery in search of the four white crosses. With any luck, the name would be there. I was almost positive it was. The part about the grave being lost didn't make much sense. Maybe she made that comment because no one visited it any more.

Out of the blue, I had a vision of a cemetery. There was a small black wrought iron fenced in area with two very old gravestones inside. The stones looked so fragile and they appeared to be leaning slightly in the uneven ground, probably due to the soil settling over the years. I got the feeling they were there for a long time. These stones partially hidden by the tall grass were the final resting places of two small girls. One of the girls seemed familiar to me, but how was that possible? Directly behind this area, stood a large tree whose significance appeared to be overpowering.

What was this all about? Was it the missing grave? Could it be a clue as to where we should search? I got the feeling I needed to investigate this place wherever it may be.

I triumphantly informed my sister about this miraculous break through. At last we had some tangible information. She said she could hardly wait to get there and check it out. She would go exploring on her day off and let me know what she discovered. I waited with profound anticipation for I feared I might never get that vision out of my head.

A few minutes later, I experienced another vision. There was an old white farm house. The roof of the front porch was lower than the rest of the structure. Some wooden chairs sat on the porch; I got a feeling the rocking chair was a special place for somebody. A very tall tree stood on the side of the house and a little picket fence surrounded the property. *Ok, now what is this all about?* The first thing that came to mind was the house must be somewhere near the cemetery. Maybe she has a view of the house from her grave. I hurried to give my sister this latest evidence. We were on a roll now.

* * *

Though it's really not a good idea to wish your life away, Tuesday night could not have arrived soon enough. My sister and brother-in-law Al drove to the cemetery that morning in search of the grave. She informed me that when she located the family plot, the wooden crosses were gone. In their place were small flat gravestones my uncle had made. They were so darling. Along with the name and date, there were tiny butterflies and stones embedded in the cement.

She looked closer and sure enough, she found the grave. The stone was only inscribed with "Elizabeth 34 years." Next to her was William, her husband. Yes, it was just like I remembered. Years ago the names didn't mean anything to me. Why would they? I was only ten. Grandma would lay flowers on the graves, but no one had ever talked about them. So I guess in a way, the graves were forgotten. Maybe that's what she meant when she said her grave was lost.

I asked my sister whether or not she saw the black wrought iron fence. She said there wasn't anything like that in the cemetery. Had she seen the white house? Again she said no. I was confused. Had I imagined the entire thing? Perhaps I was merely wishing it would look that way. After all, isn't that the type of image one might conjure up when thinking about a hundred year old grave? But then what about the house? Did I imagine that too? I know sometimes a person's imagination can run amuck.

Obviously, I was having one of those moments. Well, at least now we knew where to put those yellow flowers.

The two of us congratulated one another on a job well done. Mystery solved. Were we good or what? We triumphantly patted ourselves on the back, but the victory was short lived. A very pronounced whisper pleaded, "Please find my grave. It's lost!" What in the world was going on? In an instant, the cemetery scene flashed before my eyes again. There it was the black wrought iron fence, the gravestones, the tall grass and the big tree. "Please put some yellow flowers on my grave!" she cried.

It was at that moment when I finally understood. There was more than one person whispering to me. Although they sounded quite similar, I detected a slight difference in their voices. One of them was Elizabeth, but who was the other woman? And yet, it was as though they were both having a conversation with me about their respective graves.

Was I was getting the information confused? Were they talking to each other about the flowers? That would be interesting to say the least. For some reason I got the feeling they were. I also felt that they knew each other somehow. They didn't actually live on this earth at the same time, but they were related and found each other in the afterlife.

Who this other person was remained a mystery. Where was this other cemetery? How would I begin to find it if I didn't even know the name of the woman? All I knew for sure was that they both had a profound liking for yellow flowers. Where was the white farm house? If I could track it down, would I discover her grave? Well, Sherlock, this information wasn't going to get you very far. You're going to need a few more clues.

The days passed and I was feeling concerned and uneasy. The images of the cemetery and house continued to wreak havoc with my mind. Everything was so vivid. I could barely contain myself from sketching them over and over on my sketch pad as I became almost obsessed with it. It was all humorous in a way. That old movie came to mind where Richard Dreyfus kept drawing pictures of Devil's Tower from his dream. It was that bad. Fortunately, I wasn't trying to sculpt anything out of my mashed potatoes.

One night I had a dream that I was there in the cemetery. I had gone to Illinois to visit my sister. We drove outside of town and headed down a gravel road. There was nothing around for miles. We parked, got out of the truck and started walking. I could feel the loose gravel under my feet. The only sounds were the rocks moving as we proceeded down the road. Crunch. Crunch. We turned to the right and walked through the field. The tall grass brushed against our shoes. Snap. Snap. In my hand were those yellow flowers.

As I glanced around, there wasn't much to see. It was secluded and mostly a grassy area. But it wasn't long before I saw it. Up ahead was the small black wrought iron fence with two slightly tilted gravestones inside. Just a few feet further stood the tall tree. Under the tree was a beautiful glowing light. It was as bright as the sun and I had to squint my eyes. As I stared at it more, it appeared to be a young woman with long hair. She was wearing a blouse with a high collar and a long skirt. For a moment I thought she was a real person. Then I realized I could see through her. This had to be a ghostly apparition. She was looking at me and smiling. Our eyes met, oh those eyes, and she whispered, "You found me!"

Obviously, that was enough to awaken me from my dream. For a moment I wasn't sure where I was, but then everything came back into focus. *Ok, let's wait a minute. Shall we play back that scene one more time? On second thought, let's not. Let's take some time to wrap our head around what just happened.*

I'm not certain how the story ended. It didn't seem to matter at the moment. The mere thought of meeting face to face with a spirit again was unnerving and sent cold shivers all over my body. Something about those eyes made my mind jump back into reality. I didn't want to continue interacting with the visitation. And yes, it was not merely a dream; it was a visitation. And yet I wasn't sure why it bothered me. After all, hadn't we been exchanging thoughts for some time now? We were like old friends. I was planning to visit soon and do a little catching up. So what's the problem?

It was then that it hit me like a ton of bricks. Oh, my gosh. I felt when my sister and I set out that day, we headed down Route 6 for the infamous Troy Grove. Was it her trying to send me messages about that place for six months? Was this where the grave could be found?

"Yes, yes. Troy Grove." The voice whispered. Then the other vision appeared again. Down a gravel road was a lone white farm house with a small picket fence surrounding the yard. On the side was a very tall tree. Now what was this all about? Then just as quickly, my thoughts turned to the spot in the cemetery. Was there a connection? My head was reeling from the constant flurry of images flashing through my mind. Where was I supposed to find that house? Would the grave be somewhere nearby? Were the house and cemetery down the same gravel road? Was she the one with the graveside view of the house? *Please somebody help me solve this mystery. I'm going crazy here!* But there was no response.

Immediately, I opened my sketch pad and started to draw once again. I needed to record this while it was still fresh in my mind. That is if I was in my right mind. I don't recall ever having seen that house, but yet it seemed vaguely familiar. It felt so warm and loving inside. And there was a perfect view of the yellow flowers from the window seat by the bay window. *Oh my goodness. What are you doing INSIDE that house?* I feverously continued to draw that mysterious place portrayed in my mind. It appeared I was creating quite the portfolio for my eyes only.

Well, it was actually a relief to finally get some relevant answers. However, these were just a few pieces to a very strange puzzle. It reminded me of one of those elaborate jigsaw puzzles that were almost impossible to assemble. Half of the pieces formed the blue sky while the other half made up the blue sea and they all looked alike. They really tested ones' ingenuity. But that wasn't going to discourage me.

As a child, I would spend countless hours trying to master each one. Yes, I suppose there were other sources of entertainment a young child could have enjoyed, but spending time commanding the pieces to organize themselves kept me amused. It was exciting to watch as the pieces took shape forming a beautiful picture. I remember being quite proficient when it came to these puzzles. Defeat was not part of my vocabulary. I had never met a puzzle that couldn't be conquered. Why should this be any different? All that needed to be done was to lay all the pieces down and rearrange them enough times until I deciphered the code. The dilemma being this puzzle didn't come in a box and I didn't have the foggiest idea how the finished picture should look. Ah yes, foggy was a most appropriate way to describe it.

So where should I begin? That was the million dollar question. As luck would have it, Troy Grove wasn't a big place. Of course, the irony of it all was that a grave was missing somewhere in this small acropolis. How could this be? Surely everybody knew everybody there. Nevertheless, I was determined to get to the bottom of this. Since I lived so far away, driving around the area on my day off was not an option. I needed to explore new avenues. Maybe I could carry out some long distant investigating on the internet.

Ready or not, here I come. I promise to let no stone go unturned. Or should I say gravestone? Nervously my fingers typed "Illinois cemeteries" into the search line. Instantly, a cornucopia of information appeared before me. Which one should I choose? As my eyes perused the page, one site jumped out at me. I crossed the fingers on my left hand and clicked on it with my right. *Please tell me I'm getting warm.*

The page opened up revealing a long list of every cemetery in the state. There were even some photos. I carefully scrolled down the list. There it was, Rockwell Cemetery, Troy Grove. I had no idea there was a cemetery there. "Rockwell," she whispered. I couldn't believe my ears. *Now you're telling me? Why did you wait so long?* I waited for a reply, but nothing came.

I clicked on Rockwell to read the information and found it described as historical. Over the years the old cemetery had become abandoned, vandalized and overgrown. Most of the limestone gravestones were either destroyed or crumpled from the elements. Only a few were left standing. Even though there were many graves, most of them were unmarked. Now it was starting to make sense to me. Her grave really was lost.

Interesting enough there were some small photos. The first one showed the entrance with, oh my, a long gravel road. Somehow it looked oddly familiar to me. When the next picture came up, I couldn't believe my eyes. There was a small black wrought iron fence with two titled gravestones inside. *Are you kidding me? I sure didn't expect to see that.* Chills ran up and down my spine. That was the exact picture I had been seeing for months. I wasn't entirely crazy after all.

The mystery of the cemetery was solved. However, that would turn out to be the easiest piece of the puzzle. Now we needed to revert back to the beginning. Who was this woman telling me her grave was lost? It only seemed fitting that I know her name. After all, she knew mine.

"History," she said. *History? What does that mean?* It was very frustrating receiving only one word responses. Of course, it probably required a tremendous amount of energy to do that. Then I remembered those family tree papers. That could very well be considered history. Was that what she meant? I was sure there wasn't anything there that would be of any use. But then what would I have to lose? It wasn't as though the tip line was open and the clues were pouring in by any means. Surely, there couldn't be anything of importance there or I would have remembered.

"Of course, there is. That's how you found my name," whispered Elizabeth. I smiled and nodded my head in agreement. Well, let's open the binder and see what answers lie within the pages. There had to be one morsel of useful information there. I only needed one word. And the one I found was worth a thousand words. There was indubitably something of value there. Rockwell. The word almost jumped off the page and hit me right between the eyes. Unbeknownst to me it had been there all along.

A thirteen year old young lady named Elizabeth Trestrail from Cornwall, England died in 1880 and was buried in the old Rockwell Cemetery. At the time of her passing, the family could not provide a gravestone for her. Then over time, the cemetery had become abandoned. With the records missing, her grave was now unaccounted for and forgotten. Now what were the chances of my two ladies having the same name? And they were actually related just as I thought.

"Please find my grave," she pleaded. "It's here." Then that vision of the cemetery manifested in my mind. Forever would it be embedded in my psyche. Well, from now on, this binder would absolutely be available at a moment's notice. It had begun to serve as a treasure map of sorts. How many more stories were living within these three little pages? Somehow I knew it would be useful many more times before my family tree was completed.

So at last the cemetery was found. Now I only had to locate the grave. *But wait, it's unmarked!* Well, this will undoubtedly be a serious undertaking. After searching a few minutes, lucky me, I found a website on the internet where I could get a copy of the plots and names of everyone interred at Rockwell. *Sweet!* Without a moment's hesitation, I ordered it. Now all I had to do was wait for its arrival. *Oh, but I can't wait. I've been so preoccupied with all this for too long.*

Each day I would lay in wait for the arrival of my special delivery. I watched as the red, white and blue truck approached my street. At times, I would race my dog to look out the window, sometimes pushing him out of the way. I wasn't sure who was more excited to see the mailman. Poor Rosco would look at me as if to say, "It's all right, mommy. I've got this covered." Feeling a bit embarrassed, I agreed to back off and allow him to perform one of his favorite doggy responsibilities.

Every day after that, he stood watch by the window. When the flap on the mail box clanked, he looked over his shoulder at me. I would ask him if we got mail and he responded by wagging his tail. We were an unstoppable team.

The days seemed to drag by. Finally, I was ecstatic to be able to rescue that precious envelope from the mail box. My hands trembled as I opened the flap. Slowly, I emptied the contents of the envelope to find a letter and a check. *Wait a minute. Did they make a mistake?* The letter informed me they were returning my check as the booklet was no longer in print. How could this be? I was so close to solving my mystery. How would I ever locate the grave now? "It's right here," she said as she showed me the big tree. *Ok, Elizabeth, I believe you. We'll just have to walk the cemetery together.*

What happened next really shook me to the core. She took me back to when she was spending the night at a relative's house. They had such a great time that evening. After supper she climbed into bed and nestled snuggly under the fluffy comforter. All was well until the oil lantern over heated and the glass chimney burst. Tiny shards of glass made a tinkling sound as they fell upon the wood floor. The flames from the lantern made a mighty roar as they ignited the drapes which, in turn, engulfed the bedding. It was a sight I shall never forget. The grievous angel shed a tear over the loss of her dear friend. Then she took her gently by the hand and escorted her to a better place where her little kitten Patches was waiting for her at the gates.

Fenced in grave at Rockwell Cemetery, Troy Grove, IL

"Get your motor runnin'
Head out on the highway.
Looking for adventure
In whatever comes our way."

--- Steppenwolf

Chapter 7

The Journey

After much anticipation, the day of my journey had finally arrived. I awoke to find the morning sun anxiously peeking through my window. "Get up, sleepy head!" he called out as he smiled down on me. For a moment, I had to squint because he seemed to be especially bright that day. It was almost as though he was just as excited as I was.

As I headed out, the warm rays wrapped themselves around me like loving arms letting me know I would protected throughout my excursion. The day beckoned me to go ahead and indulge myself in the warmth and breathe in all its goodness.

It was going to be about a six hour drive. I could have very well taken a plane, but decided the trip would be more enjoyable if I convened with nature. Plus having my own means of transportation would allow me to explore at my leisure. Although at times, exploring unfamiliar territory meant getting a bit misplaced. I wouldn't call it lost. It was more like a strategically planned detour down a path not taken. And that could very well happen since I still wasn't sure where I was headed after I got to Illinois. I could only hope that no one would laugh at me for driving around in circles out on the countryside. *And no, that's not me making those crop circles.*

I couldn't help thinking how this day was going to be extraordinarily incredible. Before long I would be spending time with my distant family; some for the first time who were far more distant than I could ever have imaged. I was looking forward to indulging in my new guilty pleasure; leafing through the old musty pages at the county court house in hopes of discovering more about my ladies. What would I dig up? *Oops! That's not a good choice of words when talking about cemeteries.* All I knew was that I had a feeling it would be an unforgettable experience.

It was simply refreshing to escape the city and reconnect with nature once again. As I cruised along,

Mother Earth spread her eclectic terrain before me like a wondrous patch-work quilt. The laid-back atmosphere of the farms that dotted the countryside reminded me of a Norman Rockwell painting.

I watched as the horses were galloping wild and free through the pastures as their luxurious manes flowed in the breeze. I instantly felt like one of them, except for the luxurious mane. And cows, yes there were cows. When I saw the brown ones, I smiled remembering the chocolate milk story Grandma Alice used to tell me.

But despite the captivating view, I found the trip seemed to take a lot longer than I had anticipated. That Carly Simon song ran through my head, "Anticipation … is keeping me waiting." *Are we there yet? I'm getting tired of driving already. I've got places to go and people to see. There are yellow flowers to deliver.* Soon I realized dwelling on the time wasn't going to be very productive. Even though the minutes ticked away, the miles were not adding up. Why does it always seem to take so long to get somewhere and so quick to return home? Never could figure that one out. Anyway, I tried my best to soothe this restless heart so filled with adventure by focusing on the lovely view again instead of the odometer. Maybe that would distract me for a little longer. I had to keep reminding myself it wouldn't be long before I reached my journey's end.

In the morning, my sister and I started out on our long awaited quest. There was no road map. We embarked on our passage to the unknown armed only with the vision that would forever be embedded in my mind. We followed Route 6 leading us out of town. On the left was the Troy Grove sign. *Hey, Troy Grove. Here we come. Are you ready for us?* Up ahead on the hill the old cemetery stood proudly in the quiet solitude of the countryside. A beautiful painted sign that said Historical Rockwell 1836 greeted us. As we approached, there were butterflies in my stomach. Not being sure what to expect made me feel both excited and nervous. Would my mystery lady be patiently awaiting our arrival?

Slowly, we made our way down the winding gravel road. Tall old trees lined up like soldiers on either side of us. Were they guarding this secluded domain? Up ahead was a sign stating no visitors after sunset. *Hey, we won't have a problem with that.* We entered the gates and looked for a place to park. To the right was Rockwell with its sparsely scattered gravestones. Many had been vandalized and those that survived looked so fragile. On the left side of the road was another cemetery known as Oakwood. From my research, my Great Great Grandparents William and Alice Trestrail from Cornwall, England were buried there. Who knew? Of course, I wasn't even aware of the existence of these cemeteries until a few weeks ago for they were so far off the beaten path. It was funny, but in a strange way we were going to have a family reunion of sorts.

We got out and began to explore. The silence was eerie. I was tempted to shout out a fortuitous, "Come out, come out where ever you are!" but decided to keep it low key. The only sound of any substance was that of the loose rocks moving under our feet. Crunch, crunch. We turned and walked through the grassy area. The blades of grass brushed against our shoes. Snap, snap.

It occurred to me that everything was happening precisely according to my vision. *Yikes!* This was truly a momentous event. My sister walked over to a few of the gravestones and attempted to read the inscriptions. Some were badly worn from the elements and there was no deciphering them. I was not hopeful the one we were looking for would be found. I glanced around looking for some sort of clue as to which direction we should go.

It wasn't long before I had it in my sight. At the far end of the graveyard was a small black wrought iron fence. Knowing in my heart of hearts this was the place, I called out to my sister and we hurried over to investigate. Inside the fence were two titled gravestones. They were in somewhat better condition. However, neither name was the one we needed. We stood there a moment before I looked up. Just a few feet ahead stood a tall tree. There was nothing around except grass. However, I was convinced this was the place. How could I forget! Everything was happening exactly like in my vision. The hair on my arms began to stand up. The only part of my dream that didn't happen yet was seeing the young woman. *Please don't anybody jump out at me!* Suddenly, the silence was broken. "You found me!"

My sister didn't hear this and continued searching. She remained convinced there was a gravestone. She turned and started walking the opposite direction. Even though I sometimes question my feelings, this time I was positive about going the right way. After all, Elizabeth had shown me this location countless times. How could I not be on track? And she repeatedly iterated the fact about her grave being lost. That was probably because there wasn't a marker.

Slowly and cautiously, I proceeded forward. There was nothing but the sound of that grass brushing against my shoes. It almost echoed. For a small cemetery, it sure had good acoustics. After a few steps, I stopped and reached into my pocket. I had never used a pendulum like this, but thought it might be appropriate in this case. A pendulum is a small quartz crystal on a chain. It acts as an amplifier and can tap into energy. Perhaps it could help guide me to her vibration.

I told her we needed her assistance locating the exact spot. Holding the end of the chain with the crystal dangling, I asked her to show me what a "yes" looked like. The pendulum swirled in a clockwise circle. Then I asked what a "no" looked like. The pendulum swayed from front to back. Well, there seemed to be intelligent feedback. Hopefully it would work.

I took my first step forward. *Is your grave ahead of me?* There was a "yes" response. I moved forward a few more steps. Then I stopped and changed directions. *Is your grave ahead of me?* Again there was a "yes" response. Then a "no" response made me stop. I changed directions and repeated this several times. Suddenly, I received a "no" so I stopped. I turned left and received another "no." I turned two more times completing a square after receiving a negative response each time. What did that mean? *Am I standing on your grave?* Instantly, the pendulum whirled in a big circle. I could hardly hold it because it was spinning with such force. The air felt full of electricity and the hair on my arms was standing up. Had we actually located her lost grave? I stood for a moment and tried to recall every detail of that vision. This certainly looked like the spot where the glowing apparition was standing.

From over my right shoulder I heard an excited utterance. "Yes, yes you found me!" she shouted. *Wow that was terrifying, but mostly cool!*

I yelled over to my sister to tell her I found the grave. She came over and looked puzzled because there were no gravestones in that area. She wanted to know why I thought the grave was in that particular spot. I proudly informed her that little Elizabeth had helped guide me there. "Oh, but I'm no longer thirteen," she said. "I'm twenty years old now!"

Being satisfied that we had successfully completed our mission, we decided to call it a day. Correction, we had only completed half of our mission. Tomorrow I would have to return with those coveted yellow flowers. Before leaving, we took a few photos of the surrounding area. I was curious what might appear in them. Would we see the glowing apparition standing under the tree? Who knows what curiosity seekers may have peeked out at us from behind a tombstone. After all, they probably don't get many visitors here. Well, we will just have to change that, won't we?

Rockwell Cemetery, Troy Grove, IL

Spot under the tree where Elizabeth was buried.

"I can feel it coming in the air of the night, oh Lord.
And I've been waiting for this moment for all my life.
Oh Lord, can you feel it coming in the air of the night?
Oh, Lord. Oh, Lord."

--- Phil Collins

Chapter 8

Whispers

The following morning I bounced out of bed. I'm surprised I got any sleep at all considering all the excitement yesterday. There were so many things I still had to accomplish. First I had to go purchase those yellow flowers. They would have to be two identical bouquets. I didn't want anybody fighting over them. Now how crazy was that? Then I needed to deliver them to two different cemeteries that were on opposite ends of town. And, of course, last but not least we needed to have ample time to visit. We had a lot of catching up to do. Well, I had better get moving. Didn't want to keep them waiting any longer. They had already waited over a hundred years.

First stop on the agenda was the florist. Since time was of an essence, I was hoping to be fortunate enough to find what we needed quickly. I walked over to the cooler and happened upon a variety of bouquets. They were all so beautiful making my decision challenging. However, my two ladies were undeniably set on yellow flowers. That was very straightforward and helped me eliminate many contenders. I browsed through the cooler and triumphantly rescued two yellow bouquets. These would be perfect.

I decided to drive to St.Vincent's cemetery and deliver Grandma Elizabeth's flowers first. It was another beautiful sunny day making it a splendid time for a visit. The closer I got, the more apprehensive I became. Would she like her flowers? Would she speak to me again?

I drove down the road and entered the cemetery. *Looks like we're alone. That's good. We won't be disturbed.* I guess I was expecting some sort of response, but there was nothing. *Gee, I hope you're here after I drove all this way!*

As I turned down the lane, I found a perfect spot under the evergreen trees and parked the truck. Well, this is it. This is what we've been waiting for all this time. I anxiously stepped out and just stood there for a few moments taking it all in. The scent of pine filled the air. I liked the still and tranquil atmosphere with only the occasional cawing of a crow breaking the silence. *Of course, I don't expect total silence, right?*

I gathered the basic amenities the flowers, camera and tape recorder and turned down the row. The weather out there was a little different than in town. A soft breeze blowing through the trees made it actually feel comfortable in the 90 degree temperature especially since I did not bring a hat. Note to self: bring a hat next time. The sun reflecting off all those gravestones is hot.

As I approached the family plot, it all came rushing back to me. I had been there numerous times when I was younger helping Grandma Alice put flowers on the graves. I just never knew who these relatives were. I didn't have an inkling one of them belonged to her mother. She never mentioned her at all. In fact, I'm totally surprised she never made a comment when I decided to choose Elizabeth as my confirmation name. Coincidence? I think not.

I knelt down in the grass and touched the darling gravestones my uncle made. There were tiny butterflies and colored stones embedded in them. I looked for the names. There it was "Elizabeth 34 years." *Well, Elizabeth, here we are. I found you. So who else do we have here?* The names William and Pearl were on the adjacent stones. From my research, William was her husband and Pearl was her nine year old daughter. Now I felt sort of bad. I had only brought flowers for one grave. What to do? I decided to lay the flowers between her and her husband. That way they could both enjoy them.

At the end of the row was a stone that only said "Baby." Was I the only one that knew his name? Joseph was Grandma's first baby. He only lived a few hours. "I'm not a baby," he said. *My goodness! They're all speaking to me now.* "I'm five years old and I like trains. Can you bring me a train? *Yes, Joseph, I promise to bring you a train when I come next time.*

I had always wondered what happened to newborns when they passed. Did they remain infants or did they become young children? Obviously, my question was answered since Joseph was telling me he was all grown up. Was Grandma surprised he presented himself to her at five years when she transitioned into the afterlife? Wow, even though you get some confirmation, there are still so many questions to ponder.

I reached for my camera and took several photos of the gravestones for my family tree album. Funny but it would appear I have more photos of gravestones than living people. Then I rested the recorder down on Elizabeth's grave. I wasn't exactly sure what to expect, but I pushed record and stepped back. The recorder was the voice activated type. It only turned on when somebody spoke into it. I felt strange talking to myself, but I started to speak anyway. *Elizabeth, I brought you some pretty yellow flowers. Do you like them?* I watched the recorder turn on as I spoke and then it stopped. *I put them between you and William so you can both enjoy them. I hope that's all right.* After that I just stood there for awhile and stared at the recorder. It would turn on a few seconds and then stop. I figured it was turning on every time the breeze would blow and move the blades of grass.

After a few minutes, I bent over and picked up the recorder. I rewound the tape and listened. I didn't expect to hear anything except my voice and the breeze. "You know what? I love you," she whispered. *Oh my gosh! I wasn't alone.* Chills ran down my spine. Suddenly, I had forgotten all about the temperature.

"Did you find out anything else about her? Did you find the grave?" Was she talking about the grave in Rockwell? Had they been secretly discussing this while I was sleeping? There was something else on the tape, but the whisper was so faint I couldn't figure it out. Then I heard "Hey!" She must have been trying to tell me not to turn the recorder off. But now it was too late. Note to self: don't be in such a hurry when trying to get voice recordings.

The image of the white farm house popped into my head. So it was Elizabeth who had been planting this seed in my mind all along. I looked toward the main road and only saw a cornfield. A farm house was located at the other end of the road, but there was no chance of seeing it from where we were. And besides, it did not resemble the one in my dream. So I concluded there was no way that house was of any importance. At least, that was what I thought.

I thanked Elizabeth for the message and apologized for turning the recorder off prematurely. It was simply wonderful to actually hear her voice. I had heard it hundreds of times in my head, but this was special. I told her young Elizabeth and I had connected yesterday. The grave was no longer lost. I would be heading out there shortly.

With that, I gathered up the camera and recorder. I do believe I may have floated back to the truck because my head was in the clouds. But before I got in, I looked over my shoulder one last time. *Did that really happen?* I sat down and turned the recorder to play. Yes, it really did happen. My Great Grandmother just spoke out loud to me.

Well, one bouquet of yellow flowers had been delivered and we had a very nice chat. It was short, but so memorable. Ok, I guess it's time to head over to Rockwell. *Elizabeth, I'm on my way. Help me find the right place to put those flowers.*

As I traveled down the highway, I couldn't help but wonder if I was going to have a conversation with the young Elizabeth, too. It would be fantabulous if that happened. Yes, I made up that word. I was starting to get excited in anticipation of what was ahead. I looked over and there was the Troy Grove sign. *Hey, I'm back. I've got those flowers.* The Rockwell Cemetery sign seemed to be especially colorful today. It was almost as though it were greeting me. "Welcome, welcome we've been waiting for you. So glad you're back."

Slowly, I made my way down the winding gravel road. At the far side of the cemetery, stood the tall oak tree. I parked the truck and turned off the engine. Yesterday, my sister had joined forces with me. It wasn't until that moment that I realized I was going to be all alone. Or was I? Today it felt eerily different.

The grounds were very secluded. Tall old trees surrounded the entire graveyard like a fortress. I wondered, was it to keep people out or to keep people in? What's that line from the movie? Oh ya, "They can never hear you scream!" I looked to the right and noticed a tree had fallen. Again I wondered. If a tree falls in the graveyard, and there's no one there to hear it, does it make a sound? Or will it leave some residual energy just waiting for me to record? Ok, enough with the creepy connotations. These flowers aren't going to deliver themselves.

I reached over to the passenger side and gathered the flowers, camera and tape recorder. I removed the tape, put it back into its case and inserted a new one. Didn't want anything to happen to my precious recording. As my feet touched the ground, I could hear the gravel crunching. The sound seemed to echo.

My eyes wandered over to the other cemetery across the road. It seemed so peaceful over there. Why did this side have such an eerie feeling? Perhaps it was because it had been disturbed, vandalized and forgotten. And maybe, just maybe, they wanted to tell somebody all about it. All I knew was that I felt like I was being watched. I stood fearlessly on the road and did a 360 degree overview of the area. No, there wasn't anybody around. At least there wasn't anyone that I could see. Yet.

I turned and began my stroll through the tall grass. The blades gently brushed against my shoes. Snap. Snap. I walked past a small group of gravestones. Only one name was visible. The other inscriptions were washed out. That seemed so sad. Even though there were markers, the graves managed to hold on to their identities keeping them a secret from the world. In a way, they were lost in time. A few of the stones were broken in two. Did they deteriorate from age or did some malicious vandal willfully destroy them? It was almost as if I could feel their pain.

I approached the back of the cemetery near the big tree. I thought I saw something out of the corner of my eye. It appeared to be two women wearing long skirts. Good, I wasn't alone after all. I felt much better. I looked back at the road to see where they had parked. *That's funny, where's their car?* I looked over to the spot where they were standing, but nobody was there. *Ok, olly olly oxen free. Come out wherever you are. No, on second thought stay right there. I really have no intention of conjuring anything up.* I hurriedly grabbed my camera and snapped a few photos, but there was nothing out of the ordinary. *Well.*

Upon approaching the little fenced area, I heard a child giggle. I looked up to see the figure of a little six year old girl wearing an old fashion dress with a high collar, black stockings, black laced shoes and a big white bow in her hair. Why did she seem familiar to me? *Right, it's like you have a group of apparition friends.* Then she walked behind the gravestone and disappeared. I looked at the inscription and suddenly realized where I had seen her before. *Whoa!* She was the little girl at the Hegeler mansion that was looking at me through the fence many years ago.

Barring any more surprises, I cautiously moved forward. It was so still in the back corner I could hear myself breathing. I walked over to the landmark tree and laid the flowers down. I took a few random photos of the area. I reached for the recorder, pushed record and placed it on the special spot. *Elizabeth, I brought you the pretty yellow flowers you wanted. I'm standing on the spot that I think is your grave. Can you please come toward the little red light and speak into this box?* The recorder turned on and then stopped a few seconds later. I looked around because I had the feeling somebody was there. No, I was alone. Or was I?

Feeling hopeful I bent over, picked up the recorder and rewound the tape. What would I hear? Did she speak to me? I pushed play and listened. "I love you," she whispered. "I'll tell you this spot has my history."

I was ecstatic and in seventh heaven over finally being able to fulfill her wish. It had been a long time coming; a very long time. The adrenaline rushing through my body from these two special EVPs today made me feel intoxicated.

I promise to make you a marker and bring it back next summer when I come to town. Then everyone will be able to find your grave. I'm just sorry that you're over here all alone while the rest of your family is across the road. It felt as if she touched my hand trying to let me know she understood. It was reassuring to know.

The next summer I arrived and placed the stone on her grave. There appeared to be a special energy around that spot signifying that she was finally at peace. Every year Rockwell and St. Vincent's are my first stops when I get into town. You can never have too many yellow flowers.

Last year they arranged a heavenly surprise for me. My cousin Nancy, out of the blue, presented me with two old photos of that white farm house! It really did exist. It had been the homestead of Elizabeth's family in Granville. She had been sharing memories with me. Had it not been for these photos, I would have found myself searching forever because the house was no longer there. *Thank you, ladies.*

Great Grandma Elizabeth

Gravestone I made for young Elizabeth

Grandma Alice, GG Grandma Mary, GG Grandpa John, Pearl, G Grandma Elizabeth and G Grandpa William

O'Sadnick homestead, Granville, IL

"One of these nights
 In between the dark and the light
 Coming right behind you
 Swear I'm gonna find you
 Get ya baby one of these nights"

--- Eagles

Chapter 9

Pearl

I pulled back the drapes and gazed out upon the new fallen snow. The landscape looked simply beautiful as it glistened like diamonds under the last rays of the setting sun. He seemed to be smiling down as if he was pleasantly pleased with the canvas of the winter wonderland. Likewise, I was pleased myself; pleased that I was inside all warm and snuggly.

As usual my nightly routine would include taking my buddy Rosco by the paw and escaping into the living room. Being a connoisseur of all things edible, there were times when I would find myself over indulging. That particular evening after enjoying a wonderful Italian meal followed by a delectable dessert, my poor body bore a close resemblance to a finely stuffed Thanksgiving turkey. There would have been little chance of me trekking much further than the couch.

Luckily for me, Rosco graciously agreed to share a meager portion of the couch with me. Now at last I could pick up my feet and stretch out. *Ah, that would feel so good.* As I was about to close the drapes I caught a glimpse at the last moments of the beautiful sunset. Darkness was slowly creeping in and everything was still. A calm and peaceful feeling enveloped the room.

I reached for the remote and started to surf through the channels. What would it be? Did I want entertainment or information? And there it was, Destination Truth; both entertaining and informative. Besides my hunger for food, I always had an appetite for the unexplained. Like Josh says, "I'm not exactly sure what I'm looking for, but if it's out there, I'll find it."

It was excellent having somebody that shared a common interest. Rosco loved watching the investigations as much as I did. And somehow his little doggy watch told him when the episode was over. He waited patiently for Jason to say, "On to the next." Sometimes I thought he could see things on the screen that I couldn't. He would look over at me as if to say, "Hey that was cool. Did you see that?" At times he would look down our hallway as if he was studying something. I wasn't sure what he was looking at, but I knew Dakota visited me every day.

Try as I might, for some reason I couldn't get comfortable. *Maybe that slice of apple pie didn't require the scoop of ice cream on top. No, no, it did.* My legs kept cramping up. Every so often I would have to reposition myself. After awhile, Rosco grew tired of all the nonsense, gave me a dirty look and jumped off the couch. He circled his pillow a few times before plopping down, snuggled up and looked over at me. The unmistakable expression on his face conveyed his message, "Maybe now you can stop touching me." I nodded in agreement. I saw my opportunity to regain the coveted leg room at the end of the couch and quickly stretched out. With both of us comfortable in our new positions, we tried once more to relax.

Soon I was off on a new adventure even though I was only experiencing it from the sidelines. What was this insatiable thirst for paranormal knowledge that I found was so unquenchable? What was this preoccupation with the mysteries beyond the veil? All I knew was that each episode assured me an adrenaline rush that felt so good. Oh ya, I was captivated beyond belief.

Suddenly, there was a cold spot next to my fingers. I waved my hand around trying to determine exactly where the cold was originating. *Who's there?* I looked over my shoulder half expecting to see someone, but no one was standing there. It must have been my imagination. Talk about the power of suggestion. Feeling foolish, I reached for the blanket and covered up.

A few minutes later, Rosco lifted his head up and had a puzzled look on his face. He looked over at me as if to say, "I thought I told you to quit touching me?" I shrugged my shoulders. *What? I didn't do anything? I'm way over here on the couch.* Then he raised his paw and swatted at his head like he was trying to shoo a fly. He glanced in my direction, gave me a disgusted look and put his head back down on the pillow. Well, that was strange.

I turned back around, pulled my hands under the blanket and continued with my investigation. There were more episodes that followed. I had already seen them before, but I enjoyed watching them again. Seemed like different evidence stood out each time I reviewed them.

After getting more than my weekly fix of the paranormal, I thought it would be a good idea to call it a night and go to bed. I was starting to dose off and finding it difficult to concentrate. I motioned to Rosco and he happily led the way to the bedroom where we both climbed into bed. As I snuggled under the covers, Rosco scrunched the blanket to his liking, found his usual place pressed closely inside the crook of my knees and plopped down. It wasn't long before I was lost in dreamland.

I wasn't sure how long we had been asleep when I was jarred awake. The room had an uncomfortable feeling about it. I was lying on my side as I opened my eyes. I was startled to see a little girl standing right up by my face staring at me! *Oh, my!* She was wearing an old fashion dress and had a big bow in her hair. Having not been a sight for the faint-hearted, I proceeded to scream so loud I probably woke up the neighbors. *Now what's that thumping sound? Oh, it's just my heart.*

"You scared Pearl!" Elizabeth exclaimed. *What, I scared HER?*

"Yes, she was just watching you sleep. You screamed and scared her." Nervously, I looked toward the side of the bed, but there was no one there. I scooted over and peeked down toward the floor. Why do people always do that in the movies? It only means trouble. For sure something will jump up and grab you.

But nevertheless, I continued to lean forward. Nothing. There was absolutely nothing there. Had I imagined the whole thing? Yes, it did look like Pearl. She was wearing the same dress as in the family photo. Perhaps I was just dreaming about her. That's what you get for watching those programs last night. I looked at the clock and saw it was 4:00 a.m. *Wow, it must be Happy Hour in heaven.*

After a few minutes, I finally convinced myself it had all been a dream. There wasn't any little girl by the side of my bed. She was still sitting in the picture frame in the living room. Everything was copacetic. But as I rolled over, that song echoed in my head, "Sleep with one eye open, gripping your pillow tight." I grabbed the covers and pulled them up over my head just in case. I closed my eyes, well maybe I did keep one open, and attempted to go back to sleep. But all I could see were those eyes. I would never forget them.

Before long, the morning sun peeked from behind the drapes. I couldn't help but think that just like in the horror movies, I had survived. *My gosh. Do you have a one track mind or what? No wonder you have nightmares.* I looked around the room. Everything seemed perfectly normal. Why wouldn't it? Nothing happened last night. Or did it? I just wasn't sure.

"It really happened, "Elizabeth whispered. "She just wanted to meet you." Well, I guess I got my confirmation. But why did she wait until I was sleeping? Or was that her by the couch last night? Was she petting Rosco? I needed some convincing.

Just then I got a brilliant idea. For not being a morning person that was remarkable. I hurried to the closet stubbing my toe on the way. *Ouch!* I had completely forgotten an important rule of investigating: No running! I began to search feverishly through boxes. Somewhere in there was my little glass tea set Grandma bought for me. I thought I would give it to Pearl so she could have a tea party while I was sleeping. That way she wouldn't scare me again. Elizabeth gave me that look. *Ok, that way we won't scare each other.*

Here you are. I missed playing with you. I opened the box and carefully removed each delicate cup and saucer. I set them up on the living room table making sure all the handles were facing the same direction. That way I could tell if she moved one. *Pearl, your sister Alice gave me these pretty dishes when I was a little girl. I'm putting them on the table so you can play with them while I sleep. Then when I wake up you can visit with me. Does that sound good?* I listened, but there was no response. Hopefully she heard me. I planned on sleeping that night barring any further incident.

In the morning, I could hardly contain my enthusiasm over checking out the findings of my experiment. As I rounded the corner, my heart was pounding. I took a deep breath and glanced over at the table. Much to my disappointment the dishes were in the same place. Not one cup handle had been turned. Nor had the teapot been moved. Now I began to question myself again. Did that really happen the other night?

Feeling disappointed, I walked to the window and pulled open the drapes. The sunlight came streaming in as if to mock me and clearly reinforce the fact that nothing occurred. *Sure rub it in you and your sunny disposition.*

But as I turned and passed the table something looked out of the ordinary. In front of the tea set there appeared to be a small palm print in the dust. It was as though a child had been reaching for a tea cup. There also was something on the right side of the table. I couldn't believe my eyes. Upon closer inspection, I was astonished to see a drawing in the dust. *No, your eyes are just playing tricks on you. Or are they?*

I studied the image from several angles. It definitely appeared to be the likeness of a woman wearing a long dress sitting by a table. A little girl was leaning over the other side. Behind them was a winged angel.

"We had a tea party last night while you were sleeping, "Elizabeth whispered. "I drew you a picture." Talk about validation. Now how special was that?

I continued to leave the tea set on the table at night so that Pearl could play. One morning I woke up and found one of the cups had been moved. The handle was facing outward as if somebody had moved it; somebody that was left handed. *So you had another tea party last night I see. Hope you had fun.* For a moment I thought I heard her giggle. I didn't know if they had tea parties in heaven, but I'm glad we could have some here. I went over and straightened the cup. The next night it was moved again. Perhaps Grandma Alice was playing with her little sister and enjoying some tea parties like we used to do.

Drawing in the dust

Alice, Elizabeth & Pearl

"This is the end,
My only friend, the end.
I'll never look into your eyes again."

--- Doors

Chapter 10

Nick

The weekend was approaching and I was looking forward to attending the Mind Body Spirit Festival. The energy field at these metaphysical gatherings was always so dynamic. The experience encompassed a great array of artists, psychics, mediums, energy workers, speakers and workshops. No doubt, there would be something of interest for everyone. It was usually a memorable experience for me. I always took something home from there.

Even though I am able to communicate with spirit myself, sometimes it's a pleasure as well as helpful to have another person receive and interrupt messages for you. I know at times every day distractions get in the way. Therefore, I sometimes don't hear spirits even though they are yelling at me. Occasionally, it proves to be conducive to have another pair of receptive ears.

Looking around the room, I happened upon many familiar faces. Although we are all in the same field, each person has their own style or unique way of using their gift. All an individual had to do was determine which person connected with them the best. It seemed some people were in such demand that there was a waiting list. I didn't feel like spending the entire afternoon pacing in one place so I went in search of something different and unusual.

I strolled up and down the aisles and spied a woman sitting alone. She was a new face to the Festival. Upon approaching her, our eyes met and instantly, there was that connection. I was experiencing an overpowering feeling telling me I should stop. For some reason, there was an eerie sensation pulsing through my body indicating it would behoove me to enter into a conversation with her. There was a ringing in my right ear indicating something extremely crucial was trying to come through, but I wasn't hearing it myself.

The sign on her table stated that she would sketch a chalk drawing of the spirits around you as she did the reading. Well, now that was a new and interesting approach to mediumship. It would be fascinating to see if our supernatural information jived. There's a lot to be said for validation.

As enticing as the idea appeared to be, a little voice reminded me that the money could be put to better use. Yes, that was true. *Perhaps we should keep walking.* But before my foot could take another step, another voice, the voice of Elizabeth, whispered, "This will be money well-spent."

The woman smiled and invited me to have a seat. She encouraged me to just relax a moment while she tuned into the energy around me. A few seconds later, her fingers were rummaging through the box selecting various colors of chalk. Immediately, she put chalk to paper and began creating my story.

"There are two angels standing to your left," she began. "They are surrounded by beautiful white light." This did not come as a surprise to me. I had heard about being in the company of angels mentioned before. *Why are they there? What message do they have for me?*

"They don't have any message per se. They are merely there to offer you heavenly protection as you communicate with spirit," she said. Well, I guess that proved there was such a thing as guardian angels. And lucky me, I had two. I had always felt there was a bright light on my left side. Guess that explained it.

"As for your right side, there is absolutely somebody standing there," she said. "In fact, there is a long line of people. I can't even see the end because the line is so long. You are like a beacon attracting lost souls. They are all coming to you for help. I am going to nicely ask them to please wait their turn because I can only speak to one at a time."

That comment didn't come as much of a surprise to me either. There were moments when I could feel them lining up. At times I could even hear their feet scuffling on the floor. They would talk to me for hours. Some days the old closed sign had to be put out on the door. And yes, she was correct. Sometimes they all wanted to talk at once.

I remember the day my niece wanted me to try and communicate with her Aunt Myrtle. She attempted to step forward, but before she could speak another woman rushed up. This woman proceeded to get in front by pushing her aside and saying," Me first!" I couldn't help but laugh out loud. That goes to show you that even though our loved ones move on to heaven, they still have the same personality as they did on earth. The woman turned out to be her fiancé's Grandma and he confirmed it sounded exactly like her as she was an outspoken individual.

"There is a woman standing there," she began. I smiled and remarked it must have been my Great

Grandma. She was always there. "No, I do see her, but she has stepped aside. She's bringing another woman forward. This woman is holding her head and crying. She's been trying to talk to you for awhile." Then she paused. There was a strange and unsettling look on her face. "I don't usually tell people things like this, but she is insisting. Her husband is dead. He was murdered!"

Hold on. What did she say? Murdered? Wow, didn't see that one coming. Who was this man? Why was she trying to tell me about it? This sure was turning into a very interesting conversation. It was indeed worth every penny.

"The man is a relative. Do you know who he is? Does all this resonate with you?" she asked. I had never heard any such thing before. I asked if she could find out his name or when he was born. "I'm not sure about his name, but you do know all about him. It happened a long time ago."

This was very troublesome. Something as unique as this would be hard to forget. What did she mean when she said I knew all about him? All of a sudden the family tree popped into my mind. Are these people part of the genealogy I had uncovered? Could she tell me anything else about him?

"He's from another country and died when he was forty. One day he went to the store to buy something. He was wearing a suit. He wasn't rich, but it was a clean suit.

A man thinking he was wealthy came up and killed him for his money. Now his wife worried about what would happen to her and the children without him."

On that note, the energy slowly dissipated and she ended our session. We both agreed it was one of the most interesting yet disturbing readings ever. What was I saying about a memorial experience? This was one that would be truly unforgettable to say the least. I was anxious to return home and dive into those genealogy papers. Even though there was so much more to see at the Festival, this seemed to put a damper on things. Somehow, I knew there was nothing that could top this. With that precious drawing in hand, I bid farewell to my new friend and headed home.

The trip home seemed to take forever. I swear whenever you're in a hurry, you will hit every red light. It's a condition of Murphy's Law. I was finding it difficult to concentrate on driving. "MURDER." The sound of the word kept vibrating in my ears as if I was inside a Stephen King novel. I had to determine which one of my relatives had met with this gruesome fate at such an early age. But what was I to do with this information after I found it? I suppose spirit would let me know when the time came.

After what seemed like an eternity, I turned into my driveway. As I raced toward the door, I heard a frantic woman plead, "Please help me!" *Ok, I promise I'll do whatever I can. Just give me guidance to locate your husband. Together we can figure this out.*

Luckily, I was at the beginning stages of my family tree. My search had only taken me up two branches. I began at the most recent relatives and worked my way back. The first branch didn't contain any possible candidates. *Ok, on to the next.* Again, I started with the familiar names and moved on. Finally, there it was. I had found a man named Nicholas Trestrail who passed when he was forty. He died in 1851 in Cornwall England. His wife's name was Mary.

"Yes, yes that's him!" a distraught voice cried out. "Please help us!" *Ok, that's all fine and good, but exactly what am I supposed to do for you?* Suddenly, a gruff voice behind me shouted, "You need to tell them!" To say I wasn't expecting that would be putting it mildly. I almost jumped out of my chair. Instead of a crying woman, I was now in the company of a very angry man. The hair on my arms stood up as a negative energy surrounded me. I felt his rage and it was not good.

Is that you, Nick? Can you explain what you want me to say and who I'm supposed to tell? After I had asked the question, I wasn't sure if I wanted him to answer. He was absolutely furious and I could see him shaking. But I knew he wasn't going away any time soon. I got the distinct impression we were going to have a serious conversation.

Then as calmly as possible he showed me what happened that dreadful day.

He lived in Cornwall England. Like his father before him, he made a living as a miner. But unlike his father, he chose to sail on a ship to Cuba to work in the new Cornish copper mine called El Cobre. With the promised wages of £9 per month, he embarked on his journey. This required him to be gone for months at a time, leaving his wife and children behind. The miners found that loneliness and hard work were their constant companions. They all experienced a sense of longing to look upon the faces of their loved ones once again. However, with the decline of work in town and their thirst for adventure, they seized the only opportunity that would afford them a better life for their families.

As if working in the mine wasn't dangerous enough; they had to endure the unforgiving attitude of the mighty sea. When she was enraged, nothing was safe. She could toss the ship as if it were a child's toy. And then there was the weather which could be so unpredictable. At times the wind would howl like the Devil's own wolves. Or they could come face to face with the Devil himself while traveling in pirate infested waters. Disaster could fall upon them at any moment. It might well be the last time they would ever lay eyes on their loved ones.

On the previous day, the ship had approached Cornwall and the small village that almost appeared to be clinging to the rugged coast. It docked at the wharf not far from Redruth alongside several other vessels. After helping unload the cargo, it was finally time to head home. Nick had barely reached Fore Street when he found himself surrounded. His children had come running down the street and could not hold back their excitement. The youngest one leapt into his arms and he would have fallen backwards had it not been for a child clinging to each leg. Yes, they had missed their father. After each one had had the opportunity to hug him, they continued down the street to their house. Everyone was trying to speak at the same time which made it difficult to understand one word. Nick merely smiled.

Exhausted and dirty he walked toward the door. Before he could reach for the handle, it swung open. At last, there stood his lovely wife Mary. She looked like an angel as the sunlight lit up her face. Despite his ruffled appearance, she reached her loving arms out and hugged him. Somewhere from deep inside, a new found surge of energy emerged and he squeezed her as tight as he could. He remarked that he must be quite the sight. She smiled and said, "You're the best sight in the world!"

After that wonderful homecoming and a good night's sleep in his own bed, he had something important to do. He headed into town listening to the familiar sound of the wooden walkway as it creaked beneath his feet. It was a peaceful afternoon only interrupted by the occasional squawk of seagulls or the sound of the waves as they lapped against the dock. The tin roofs of the small shops begged to gleam in the sunlight. But instead, the fog was rising up from the sea drifting over the wharf and the cobblestone streets. The distinct aroma of the salty sea filled the chilly air. Nevertheless, it would be a good day to browse through the merchant's wares.

After leaving the shop, Nick stopped for a moment and stood on the walkway. He wore a brown suit. It wasn't expensive, but it was neat and clean. In his wallet was a small amount of money he had managed to put aside from his meager miner's wages. In the other pocket was a necklace the store clerk only moments before had carefully wrapped in paper. It was their anniversary. He wanted to surprise his wife.

He stood there, his heart brimming over with love, never suspecting the danger creeping in. The seagulls were silent perhaps sensing the dark energy in the air. Animals seemed to have a way of knowing such things. The sea was now perfectly calm and its murmurs barely audible.

A short thin man stood in the shadows watching him. He wore a tattered shirt, dark pants and a cap. He was one of the town thieves. Sadly, he was very proficient at the unspeakable deeds he carried out. Thinking that

Nick was a wealthy man because he was wearing a suit, the man lay in wait. When the opportunity arose, he quietly moved into position. He pulled out a long shiny knife and with great precision proceeded to stab Nick in the back. The icy cold blade traveled deep into his heart. He grabbed his chest, blood gushing everywhere and gasped for air. He tried to breathe, but only choked on his blood. He began to stagger and again down came the blade this time piercing his lung. As his heart cried out its last beat for his beloved Mary, he slumped to the ground. The thief grabbed his wallet, but failed to look into the other pocket that held the precious necklace. He quickly became one with the shadows and was gone. Sadly, he was never apprehended.

"You need to tell them!" he vehemently exclaimed. "They need to know what happened!" He was so adamant about it that he was clenching his fists. There was fire in his eyes. I had never encountered an angry spirit before. How was I to handle this? Since we were related, I was hoping we could come to an amiable conclusion. *Nick, I'm sorry about what happened to you. But I don't know what to do. That was 160 years ago. Who am I supposed to tell? What can anyone do now?*

I waited for a response, but now it was quiet. The room felt calm again. He was gone. I wasn't sure where he went or if he would return. All I knew was that I was totally drained after that. Perhaps a good night's sleep would help. In the morning, I could try and figure out how to make Nick feel better, if that were at all possible.

The following day, the morning sun was shining through the window with the promise of a better day. I felt fully refreshed and rejuvenated. It's amazing what some rest will do for you. Now that I had a clear head so to speak, I needed to digest all the events of yesterday. It was truly a lot to comprehend. MURDER. The poor man was murdered. I could only hope he felt better now that he told somebody.

Today would be a good day to continue researching. Maybe I could uncover more information about Nick's family. What happened to them after he was gone? Hopefully they were all right.

I walked over to the computer, but excuse the expression, stopped dead in my tracks. *What the heck is going on? Who did this?* There was a cute little pewter angel on my key ring. Her head was attached to the ring. However, her body was on the other side of the table. Somehow her head had been savagely torn off. How did this happen? This was pewter a virtually indestructible metal and it couldn't just break.

A cool chill ran throughout my body from head to toe as my eyes nervously surveyed the room. Nothing else appeared to be out of place. Who was I kidding? There was only one logical explanation. I was hesitant, but needed to ask. *Who did this? I want to know right now! Speak up!*

"I did it!" the familiar gruff voice called out. "I bloody told you to tell them! Now are you going to do it?" Well, well look who's back. Talk about your unwanted house guests. And wasn't it just my luck, a spirit with attitude. This was going to require some special handling.

Nick, you are not allowed to touch me or anything in my house. Understand? Why did you break my favorite angel? "I don't know. I was mad," he grumbled. "I just want you to tell them what happened."

Ok, remember what I told you? This all happened 160 years ago. There's not much the authorities can do about it now. How about if I tell our relatives the story? Will that make you and Mary feel better?

"I guess that will be good. I just need somebody to know what happened to me. I don't want people to forget," he said. As soon as he said that, I could feel his anger subside. He was starting to calm down. I thought perhaps I saw him smile a little even though I was sure he'd deny it.

During the next few weeks, I conveyed his amazing story to several relatives and friends. Incredible information like that would never be found on any genealogy site. According to census records, Mary somehow managed to overcome the ugliness of that fateful day. She never remarried perhaps because she continued to hold on to that necklace and the memory of her dear Nicholas. She kept the seven children with her instead of putting them into an orphanage as sometimes happened. Hopefully, I had remembered every detail as I related the story each time. Afterward, I asked him if I had done a good job. He just smiled.

Cornwall, England
Photo by Darren Strick

Angel key chain

"The sky is crying.
Can't you see the tears roll down the street?"

--- Stevie Ray Vaughn

Chapter 11

Anne

A few years ago, my friend Sue in Illinois proudly announced she was going to partner with somebody and open a salon. They were both head over heels excited about entering into a new venture. After having leased a prime location, there were a few more particulars that needed attention such as remodeling and decorating.

Every few days or so, she updated me on how the renovations were progressing. Then I provided her with a few updates of my own. One night I had a vision known as remote viewing. I saw her diligently painting the salon. Michelangelo would have been proud. Layers of drop cloths surrounded the room as she popped open cans of latex. The distinctive essence of Dutch Boy filled the air as she poured the contents into the tray and proceeded to slide the roller around. Stopping only for the occasional coffee fix, the two women put heart and soul into the transformation. The blond woman standing next to her commented on how much she loved the color selection. The following night I saw the salon completed to perfection and open for business. Sue was styling a client's hair and the blond woman was standing next to her again. This had to be her new partner although she didn't mention her name.

Suddenly, I had a brilliant idea. Why not design some necklaces for her and the partner? They would have crystals and charms characteristic of a stylist such as a brush, comb and hair dryer. That would be something fun and a great conversation item they could wear at the Grand Opening. I could even make variations of the idea to have available for sale to clients.

I sent Sue a photo of the prototype. I asked her which color crystals she preferred for herself. Did she think that would be something they would both like? She replied saying she thought it was a clever concept, make her blue and advised me to go ahead with the production. However, even though she would adore one, she didn't believe her partner would be too keen about the idea. *Why wouldn't she? What's not to like about those darling jewels?*

She suggested we come up with something else for her partner because jewelry was not their cup of tea. The reason being was because her partner was a man. *Man? Then who was the blond woman standing there? I saw her plain as day in both visions.* Sue just laughed sarcastically and said, "Maybe she's a ghost."

Well, wasn't that interesting? I could clearly see this woman interacting in harmony with the people around her. As my friend was working her magic on the client's hair and engaging in a jovial conversation, this woman was laughing along with them. On another occasion, the two of them were standing in back enjoying a cup of coffee. If she was only there in spirit, it was remarkable how content and comfortable she was with the living.

But as I carefully critiqued the details, I began to have second thoughts. Something was not quite right. At first I couldn't put my finger on it, but then I realized what it was. Even though she appeared to blend in well with the surroundings, her hair style and clothing seemed out of place. Clients rely on their stylist to be a trendsetter and keep them in vogue. Something about her reminded me of the eighties. She had that big hair with feathered bangs and round wire rim glasses. And, oh my goodness, her jacket had padded shoulders. Yes, she definitely was from another time period. *I wonder how far a commute she had.*

Well, that settled it. Now I had to learn who this mysterious silent partner was and why she was still on payroll. Guess the only way to unearth the information was to ask her. *Hi there, excuse me for infringing on your privacy and disrupting your day. I was noticing you hanging around the place. You aren't from around here are you? Can you tell me your name and something about yourself?*

With that I received an instantaneous response. Yes, as a matter of fact, she was from around there. She smiled, removed her wire rim glasses and said her name was Anne. Not too long ago in a previous life this building was an office. She used to work there and apparently still did. I saw her seated at a desk up front that was located behind a counter. She had pursued a career as a receptionist with a propensity for clearly taking charge of the office. Resolving issues, answering the phone, filing and greeting clients were her forte. She adored her job and nothing would deter her from getting to work. And fashion, oh fashion was so very quintessential to her. It was reflected in her choice of hair style and clothing. She was a fashionista, even though I don't believe that word was around back then.

But what happened to you? Why are you still here? She sighed and walked to the back of the salon. She reached over for the coffee pot and slowly poured herself a cup. Oh, how she loved coffee. She couldn't get enough of that robust brew. Then she shared her story.

It was a typical frosty winter evening. However, the weather forecast warned of freezing conditions. As the snowflakes softly swirled across the road, the small blue car made its way through the shadows of night. The wisps of white resembled hundreds of tiny skaters holding hands and playing crack-the-whip. Her sister was driving and she was seated on the passenger side. Anne didn't fasten her seatbelt because she didn't want to wrinkle her outfit.

They started down the winding curves heading into Spring Valley. The lights of the city twinkled in the distance. They turned on the radio, but couldn't agree on the station. Anne wanted to listen to Christmas music, but her sister wanted rock and roll. One thing they both agreed upon was the fact that they were inside safe and snuggly. They had successfully made it to the car without a hair out of place. It was all about the hair.

Anne asked her sister if she remembered how they used to go caroling when they were in grade school. She nodded and said they should do it again sometime. Anne laughed and remarked that they had better practice first. She leaned in and searched for a Christmas station. Soon the sisters were singing in perfect harmony, "All is calm. All is …."

Suddenly, without warning they came upon black ice. The car started to slide and began to spin. The woman gripped the steering wheel with all her might, but was no longer in control. Everything began to move in slow motion. Panicked screams pierced the night air. Seconds later the car catapulted into the side of the concrete wall. Anne felt the sensation of the glove compartment as it pressed against her kneecaps crushing them. Her petite body was tossed about like a rag doll. Sparks were flying as metal scraped against concrete. The sound of metal twisting and breaking and the tinkling of broken glass reverberated through the darkness. The sisters frantically reached for each other's hands. Then there was only silence as the car came to a stop. The stillness seemed almost deafening.

Through the plumes of smoke rising from the disabled engine, it appeared the driver sustained several cuts and bruises. The passenger side received the most damage. I could feel the excruciating pain in Anne's chest as she gasped her last breath. Snowflakes gently covered her with a loving blanket. The city lights up ahead were almost afraid to shine after losing one of their own.

* * *

Even after relating that horrific story to my friend, she remained somewhat skeptical. After all, she was not a believer of the paranormal. But how could I have imagined all this? Surely she could keep an open mind and explore the possibilities. So on my next trip to Illinois we planned a little day time investigation in hopes of turning her into a believer. Since the salon was closed on

Mondays, that seemed to be the perfect opportunity to have our meet and greet with our mysterious lady.

My sister Cathy, Sue's friend Ari and her mom would be joining us that afternoon. One of my other sisters enlightened me about the building's history. It used to be among other things an insurance office and her agent was Steve Kaufmann an old college classmate of mine. Well, that was an interesting tidbit. I could hardly wait to ask Anne if we had a friend in common. That would be a unique friendship to share.

Monday afternoon we gathered at the salon feeling giddy with excitement. Sue was not convinced we would be successful in contacting anyone because it was daylight. The guys on television always conducted their investigations at night. *Really? So you admit to watching these programs? Maybe you aren't as skeptical as you think.*

My sister and I glanced at each other with one of those knowing looks. Not too long ago we had some very impressive encounters in the middle of the afternoon. We were attempting to communicate with the spirits at two abandoned cemeteries and were quite successful. Sue being fraught with uncertainty wanted to hear proof of our experience since she was convinced spirits only wandered cemeteries at night. We were certain today would be the most opportune time to prove this otherwise and promised to share our findings with her right after we visited with her lady.

So yes, I was confident this beautiful day would not disappoint us. I placed the recorder and K-II meter on the shelf next to the mirrored wall. The K-II is a small hand held device with five LED lights. It is used to measure fluctuations in electromagnetic fields. This is referred to as EMFs. It is said that spirits produce their own electromagnetic impulses and are able to manipulate it at will. Their strength is measured by lighting up a sequence of colored lights.

As we began to try and converse with our lady, I also took some random photos of the room. With all eyes waiting in anticipation for a light fluctuation, I asked that important question, "Anne, do you know Steve Kaufmann?" Unfortunately, none of the lights lit up.

After a few more minutes of questions and virtually no response from the K-II, Sue remarked, "Either there isn't any ghost here or you don't know what you're doing. The ghost hunters on television would have found something by now." *Oh no, you did not go there!*

With everyone now staring at me and obviously scrutinizing my every move, I needed to be ready with my explanation. "Well, since inquiring minds are demanding to know, I'll have to expound on some misunderstood conceptions. It takes the investigators many hours and sometimes days to finally come up with the few minutes they present on television. Sometimes they don't find any evidence. And last, but not least, spirits do not 'perform' on command because, after all, they are real people like us. If they don't feel comfortable, they are not going to interact."

Hopefully now everyone understood the gist of the matter. By the smiles on their faces, I knew they did. Then Ari, who was almost speechless, pointed behind me. The hand held mirror hanging from a hook on the counter was swaying back and forth. We tried several times to recreate the action, but the mirror never moved. Had it been our lady responding in agreement to my little speech?

Thank you so much, Anne for letting your presence be known. I knew you were here.

At that moment, Ari who also has abilities, sensed the presence of a woman in the room. I had disclosed very little information before hand, not wanting to sway her in a certain direction or in any way distort the facts. Hoping to have her reinforce my initial findings, I asked if she could describe the lady. Sure enough she reinforced what I had seen to the letter.

I picked up the recorder, rewound and pushed play. Unbeknownst to us, Anne had been communicating with us all along. When asked if she knew Steve, there was a resounding, "No!" I was excited that she was responding to us, but at the same time a little disappointed. We were wishing she worked with Steve so we would be able to ask him some questions. But now we were back to square one. And it appeared our session had ended. She had most likely used every bit of her energy to move that mirror. Perhaps, someday soon we would solve the mystery.

I looked at Sue and asked, "Well, now are you a believer? Do you think there really is a spirit hanging out in your salon?" She nodded her head in agreement. "And somehow we did this in the middle of the afternoon," I sarcastically remarked. "So now is everyone eager to hear our tales of the abandoned cemeteries?" Sue just smirked back at me.

Spring Valley hill

"Help, I'm steppin' into the twilight zone.
This is a madhouse, feels like being home.
My beacon's been moved under moon and star.
Where am I to go now that I've gone too far?

--- Golden Earring*

Chapter 12

Lithuanian Liberty Cemetery

Spring was well underway bringing forth the promise of new life and new beginnings. The countryside flourished with wild flowers and fields of grain resembling a beautiful patch-work quilt. Just before the Spring Valley curve shrouded within a wooded area is the Lithuanian Liberty Cemetery. There is little hope of new beginnings here or what most people would consider living. There is only the notion some people entertain about a thing called the afterlife.

This small graveyard, ranked number two on the Illinois Haunted Cemetery List, consists of thirty gravestones and one mausoleum belonging to the Massock brothers. The locals refer to the grounds as the Massock Cemetery.

In the 1960's, some teenagers looking for thrills vandalized the grounds, unearthing graves and breaking into the mausoleum. They desecrated the remains of one of the three brothers entombed in the structure. One boy stole his skull and morbidly displayed it on the handle bars of his bike as he road back to town. When law enforcement realized the skull was human, they returned it to the family who placed it back inside the mausoleum. In order to prevent any further transgressions, the doorway was cemented shut to keep intruders from entering. But did it prevent anyone from leaving?

Legend has it a hatchet man wanders the graveyard. Is it the spirit of the former caretaker of the Massock mansion who killed his wife with an axe and buried her under the building? Or is it another resident performing his duty as neighborhood watch? Whatever the case, there is no doubt the spirits are restless after such unprovoked and ghoulish attacks.

After my cousin Terri shared her personal experiences with us, we could not discount the legend and approached the cemetery with high expectations. But finding the graveyard would prove to be an arduous task. When people allude to it as hidden, they aren't kidding. After driving along the small stretch of road several times, we finally located what appeared to be a gravel entrance. Amidst the tall overgrowth was a barely visible old chain stretching across a grassy pathway.

I parked the truck on the shoulder and crossed the road. Surely this had to be the spot. Like a ninja I slowly crept up to the ominous portal and peered inside. Once my eyes adjusted to the fluctuation in light, I could see we were in the right place. I motioned my sister to join me and we climbed over the old chain. But before we could begin our investigation, there was one small matter to deal with; the police car that had unexpectedly pulled up behind mine. *Yikes, busted!*

I turned to find the officer writing down my plate number. A myriad of thoughts ran through my mind as I reluctantly approached him. *Should I not have parked there? Were we not supposed to enter the cemetery? ... Bad boy, bad boy what you gonna' do?* The officer looked up, noticed me and asked if it was my vehicle. He observed the out-of-state plates and wondered if it had broken down or was abandoned. I assured him everything was fine and we were merely going to explore the cemetery. *Was that ok?*

Without acknowledging my question, he asked for my license and registration and returned to his car to verify the information. It seemed to take forever as he ran the search. All the while I stood there feeling like a child being caught after they were told to stay in their own yard. *But they were calling me to come play.*

Finally he returned from the police car and handed back my identification. "Here you go," he said. "Have fun investigating, but make sure you're out before dark. We don't allow anyone in the cemetery at night for obvious reasons."

"Oh, don't worry we have no intention of engaging with the residents in the dark," I replied. "Have you ever visited the cemetery?"

"No, I have not and there is no way you would get me in there," he laughed. "All I can say is have fun, but be careful." With that, he got into his car, waved to us and headed down the road. *Well, wasn't that an interesting comment?* This small unassuming cemetery was really beginning to peak my curiosity.

Once inside we were surrounded by a fortress of tall trees that not only guarded the perimeter, but also extended their branches to form a canopy above us. Yes, it was as though we had entered into another dimension closed off from the world we knew. We felt as if we were inside a vacuum void of sound. The silence was almost deafening. It seemed like dozens of eyes were engaged in penetrating stares. Were we on display for the spirits to observe? Were we truly ready for this dubious undertaking? It was too late to look back. Whatever had beckoned us had already held us captive.

We entered the graveyard with high hopes of being welcome. *Hey, sorry to drop by unannounced. Hope it's ok.* As I suspected the grounds were in complete disarray. Many of the stones were broken or knocked over. There were several unmarked sunken burial sites with only a cement curb surrounding them. Toward the back stood the old mausoleum. It almost looked like a castle standing proudly in its kingdom. It was sad seeing how the doorway had been sealed shut on the beautiful memorial.

We slowly walked around reading the inscriptions while occasionally pausing to look over our shoulders. Although there was nothing unusual for the eye to see, you could feel a presence around you. I began singing, 'Lunatic fringe, I know you're out there!" Suddenly, there was a rustling sound behind us. Snap! Snap! We stopped and looked around the cemetery, but there was nothing. Or was there? My ears were at attention, but the only detectable sound was the reverberation of my heartbeat anticipating danger. *Hello, we come as friends. Please don't be afraid.*

We moved to the center of the grounds and decided it would be a perfect place to try and communicate with whoever was following us. I sat down on a base that once supported a gravestone. My sister chose another one in front of me. I turned on the Spirit Box and set it down. This device is a modified digital radio. It uses radio frequency sweeps that scan over various radio stations at 100 milliseconds to generate white noise. It is believed this provides spirits the energy they need to be heard.

A lone butterfly flittered past us and came to rest on the same base only a few inches away from me. He remained there for about fifteen minutes. It seemed he did not mind the Spirit Box. Or was it he that was trying to communicate with us? Cathy turned and asked me if I had just touched her right shoulder, but it was not me. She was sure she felt the sensation of fingertips. Guess it was time to find out what was going on here.

I just put a small black box on the stone. You can use this to speak to us. Can you tell us who just touched her shoulder?

"John"

Did you send this butterfly?

"No"

Did you live in Spring Valley?

"I did ... for years."

Did you know my relatives the Seabecks?

"Yes"

Are you the one known as the Hatchet Man?

"No"

Is he here?

"No"

Were you a miner? My Grandfather was a miner.

"No"

Were you a farmer?

"No"

What was your job?

"Roads"

Is it ok that we're here?

"I guess"

How many people including us are here right now?

"Seven"

Does anyone want else to speak with us?

"No"

Ok, thank you for talking with us. We are going to walk over to the mausoleum. Can you come with us?

"Ok"

I reached over and carefully retrieved the Spirit Box because our butterfly friend was still hanging around. I never did figure out why, but felt a loving presence around him. I wondered who the other spirits might be. Perchance they were just as curious to see us as we were to see them. Maybe they were being cautious about approaching us wondering if we were trust worthy or foolish like the others.

We made our way over to the mausoleum wondering if John had accompanied us. Legend has it the temperature of the doorway is always warmer than the rest of the structure. I had to find out for myself. We both felt the cemented doorway and the sides of the tomb. Sure enough, the door was quite warm while the sides were cool to the touch. I checked the surfaces with my meter and there was a significant difference. I wasn't sure what to make of it since we were clearly in the shade, but it was interesting.

My curiosity got the best of me as I decided to look through the small vent on the side. This is one time where being tall came in handy. My sister was afraid somebody might be looking back at me, but if they were it was too dark inside to tell. Suddenly, we heard a faint growl. Perhaps it was best to leave the mausoleum alone. Instead, I decided to sit down on the step in front and conduct another Spirit Box session.

Can I sit here?

"No!"

Why not?

"Oh, I guess"

Can you tell me the name on this mausoleum?

"Massock"

How many people are in there?

"Four"

Can you tell me what month this is?

"June"

What day is it?

"Tuesday"

Did you know the Seabecks? They were my relatives.

"Yes"

That's great. Do you have anything else you want to say?

"No … nothing"

Ok, well I have only one more question. John, can you tell us your last name and if you have a grave here? Unfortunately, our mysterious grounds keeper did not answer. We took one final tour around the cemetery searching for any indication of John, but could not locate him. Was he one of the unfortunate souls forever lost in time having been buried in an unmarked grave? Why does he remain here?

Perhaps we could have another conversation next time I'm in town.

Lithuania Liberty Cemetery, Spring Valley, IL

"I looked around
And I knew there was no turning back.
My mind raced
And I thought what could I do.
And I knew
There was no help, no help from you."

--- AC/DC

Chapter 13

Bachelors Grove Cemetery

Amidst the daily hustle and bustle of the big city is a place where some pay no mind to the ticking of the clock. Day softly fades into night with nary a sound in this quiet alcove that time has forgotten. Near the Rubio Woods Forest Preserve, along a section of the old Midlothian Turnpike lies Bachelors Grove Cemetery, one of the oldest pioneer cemeteries in Cook County.

Soon after the Black Hawk War of 1832, many Natives surrendered their land in Northern Illinois. Those remaining found immigrants arriving from Ireland, Scotland, England and Germany hoping to claim timberland on which to build their homesteads.

The origin of the name is debatable. Some believe it refers to the many single men who first settled there and died during the construction of the Illinois-Michigan Canal. Death records contain variations of the name perhaps depending on the recorder's phonetic interruption since the level of education at that time was basic; Batchelders, Batchelors and Bachelors.

However, one thing is for certain, during the early 1800's, it was customary to name a stand of timber after the immigrants who settled there. Records indicate a German family named Batchelder purchased 80 acres for the price of $200. Other documents suggest this particular parcel changed ownership several times: Smith, Everdon and Schmidt. This attributed to the variance in cemetery names listed on death certificates; Smith and Everdon Cemeteries are often listed along with Bachelors Grove depending on the time period.

Nevertheless, the acre of land designated to be used as a graveyard for family and neighbors now bore the name Bachelors Grove. The first known burial was in 1823 and the last in 1965 with a total of about 150 interments. The grounds were once a peaceful park where families would come visit the graves of their loved ones. They would spend a Sunday afternoon enjoying picnics under the shade of the trees or fish and swim in the small nearby pond. But the once tranquil sanctuary, had succumbed to many disruptive forces.

In the 1920's, it was said the infamous mobster Al Capone who had a house nearby, would use the pond as a dumping ground for his victims. Police searches recovered twelve bodies and several firearms possibly linked to the war over liquor traffic during Prohibition. Two victims at a house down the road were found riddled with bullets from a machine gun. During the 1960's, the graveyard was vandalized unearthing wooden coffins, desecrating remains and destroying or stealing gravestones.

It was not unheard of to wake up and find a gravestone unexpectedly deposited in your front yard. Even after the tedious task of transporting them back to the cemetery, many of them found their way out again. Locals began joking about the powers of the mysterious disappearing-reappearing gravestones. However, the souls of the Grove did not take it so lightly. Since then the historical cemetery has been ranked number one on the Illinois Haunted Cemetery List and is among the most haunted in America.

We parked the truck outside the Forest Preserve. While other visitors headed down the familiar path, we chose to take the one seldom traveled. Our journey was not as easy since our destination was located across an extremely busy road. Not having the luxury of a cross-way, we were at the mercy of the relentless traffic whizzing by. After dodging around several vehicles, we found ourselves momentarily marooned on a narrow gravel strip. We were surrounded by an endless barrage of steely eyes and shiny teeth just waiting to take a bite out of us should we dare step foot into their path. The force of the wind ricocheting off the speeding traffic blew ripples through our t-shirts. We felt as though we were engaged in a game of dodge ball and the other team was out for blood.

Finally, there was a reprieve and we managed to make our escape to the other side. We climbed over the rusty cable stretching across the remains of the old Bachelor Grove Road, rerouted in 1960, that was now silent and forgotten swallowed by the forest around it. Once inside the fortress of tall trees, we immediately sensed an eerie feeling. It seemed quite different compared to the woods across the road which was so full of life with chirping birds, butterflies and dragonflies. Instead it felt stagnant and full of death.

On the left, were the remnants of an old foundation. Tiny bits of pottery and glassware are still scattered about. A plot survey indicated there were once three houses along the road; the Schmidt house less than 300 feet from the cemetery. About a quarter of a mile down the road, a tall chain link fence keeping vigil over its many souls emerged from the clearing. We discovered the gates of the graveyard propped open. Were they welcoming strangers with open arms or tempting them to unwittingly enter this forsaken place? Although I had longed to investigate there for many years, I wasn't sure which one to believe. However, there was no turning back for she was undeniably holding me in her clutches and luring me toward her kingdom.

Various stories had been reported over the years. Supposedly, a nearby farmer was plowing his field. The horse was spooked and began to run toward the water. Unable to control the animal, the man became entangled in the reins and dragged into the pond where they both met with a watery death. Witnesses claim to have seen a ghostly horse emerge from the pond pulling a plow and a man. Just inside the gates is the Patrick family gravestone. It is said that this stone mysteriously moves about the cemetery as it is often found in another location. There is also the 1991 photo of the ghostly lady in white referred to as the Madonna who was seen sitting on a gravestone. Sometimes she is heard crying as she wanders. Is she searching for her baby? Put that together with disembodied voices and unexplainable lights and it is the perfect recipe for a haunted cemetery.

As we entered the gates, a hint of loneliness surrounded us like a low hanging fog. Traces of grief, despair and unimaginable sadness lingered in the stillness of the afternoon air. What lay before us was disheartening. Most of the gravestones had been destroyed and the entire notion of serenity had been disrupted. Some markers were hidden behind overgrowth while remnants of others jutted out of the earth. It seemed only the mightiest remained perhaps because they were too large to carry away. What once was the final resting place for these pioneers had now become the grounds of unrested peace.

We slowly walked around searching for any sign of intact gravestones. There were actually quite a few. Most of the older ones were located near the entrance. As we read the inscriptions, we couldn't help but feel sad wondering how many more graves at the hands of vandals were now unmarked and forever lost in time.

With cameras in hand, we separated and headed in opposite directions. While snapping some random photos near a huge monument with the name Fulton, I felt a presence. Suddenly a disembodied voice, a vocalization that does not require recording devices, but is audible to the human ear, called out, "Mommy!" I spun around thinking I would see a little girl, but there was nothing there. Next to the gravestone was a small marker with the words "Infant Daughter" on it. From my research I found it was the grave of baby Marci May. Near the base were numerous coins that previous visitors had left behind for her. Was she still looking for her mommy?

My sister called out and motioned for me to join her over by the fence. She told me to look back in the trees behind the cemetery where we both witnessed a strange light. It appeared as though it was a lantern shining, but it was the middle of the afternoon and we thought there was no one else around. Then it just disappeared. We turned and began to walk away when we heard another disembodied voice, "Hey, come back here!" Startled, we did an about face expecting to see an actual person on the other side of the fence, however no one was there. She knelt down, brushed away some grass and uncovered the crumbing remains of a flat gravestone. We searched for the inscription, but it had worn away long ago forever holding the name no more than a memory. What was he trying to tell us? Was he the one shining the light in the woods?

I decided to walk outside the cemetery gates to make sure there wasn't anyone further down the pathway. In the distance I could see a two story Victorian white farm house with wooden columns in front. There was a porch swing, white picket fence and a light in the window. But why were the lights on? It was remarkable to see since I was not aware of any structures in the area. We were after all, in the woods. I called to my sister so that we might go explore my find. But when I turned back around, the house had vanished. I had not been aware that day of the story about the phantom house randomly appearing and disappearing. It was both exciting and an honor to be one of the lucky people experiencing the phenomena. Was it somebody sharing the memory of their home with me? Were they recalling a much happier time? Was it the mysterious soul buried near the fence?

We approached the square basket-weave stone where the apparition of the infamous seated Madonna was photographed. It is said this is the spirit of Amelia Patrick Humphrey. She lost her first child Libby May at the age of eleven months. I snapped several photos in hopes of capturing her, but was unsuccessful. I decided to sit on the stone myself and see if I could feel her presence. *Hope you don't mind me being here. I would love if we could visit for a while.* The stone was cool to the touch. I gently slid my fingers along the intricate pattern on the side imagining how beautiful the original must have been.

Soon a wave of sadness and loss pulsed through my body. Were these the residual emotions of a mother mourning the loss of her child? Was she wondering if by turning back time she could have changed everything? Oh, that she could hold her precious little one for just a little longer, see her smile and hear her laugh once again. Oh, if only that were possible, but alas, all she had to hold on to were memories. Have these feelings of incompleteness caused her to wander the cemetery all these years?

I decided to walk back over to the Fulton gravestone where I had heard the voice a few minutes ago and try a Spirit Box session. *Is there anyone here who would like to speak to us? If so, please come over to this little black box I have in my hand and use it to talk to me.*

Within seconds I heard, "Mommy" ... "Come play" I was excited as it seemed my little girl had returned. Then I felt a gentle tug on the bottom of my shirt as if a small child was trying to get my attention.

Who are you?

"Me"

Ok, where are you?

"Hide"

Why are you hiding from me?

"Come play"

But I can't find you. Can you come out so I can see you? Olly-olly-oxen free. I waited, but unfortunately, my little friend did not come out of her hiding spot. She was obviously very good at this game.

Is there anyone else that would like to speak with us before we leave? I patiently waited, but there was no response. We wondered if perhaps it was now their quiet time and they wished to be alone.

We kindly thanked the spirits for allowing us to visit and headed out. As I walked past the gates, I paused and looked over my shoulder for one last glimpse of the mysterious grove. This was not good bye of that I was certain because I knew we would be meeting again.

Strange light in the woods near the gate

Madonna Stone

Bachelor's Grove Cemetery, Midlothian, IL

Marci Mae Fulton grave

"Count the stars in a summer sky
That fall without a sound.
And then pretend that you can't hear
These teardrops comin' down."

--- Poco

Chapter 14

Sarah

One day I came across an article about William Ganong Cemetery that peaked my interest. In 1832, he designated a portion of his farm land as a cemetery for his family and neighbors. The graves numbered 353, although some of them were unmarked. Supposedly there were sightings of a woman in white who would wander the grounds. Legend has it that she would cross the road in the darkness of night. Drivers assuming she was real would swerve to avoid hitting her. This story sounded very intriguing to me so I thought I would go investigate.

Over the years, the cemetery had become overgrown and unkept. Many of the older fragile gravestones had been vandalized. The grounds had now been cleaned up and the stones pieced together. I wasn't sure why, but I had a feeling I needed to go there.

When I first arrived, I was in awe with its beauty. I found it amazing how the cemetery was carved into the side of a grassy hill. I entered the huge iron gates and followed a winding gravel road that twisted its way through the graveyard. There were two elevations, but the road only allowed access to the lower grounds. In order to reach the top, you had to walk. Or should I say climb? How in the world did they carry the coffins up there?

I wanted to study the immediate surroundings along the road to the cemetery. What or who was actually responsible for the accidents? Was there a ghostly apparition crossing the road or did it have something to do with driver error? I drove south on the road a bit and then turned around. On my way back, I noticed how the road suddenly turned into a sharp curve. There were dense trees and bushes on either side. When the road finally straightened out, I was directly in front of the iron gates. However, I also observed that an apartment complex was on the other side. Could it be when a car came around the curve they became startled by a real person in the road? Or perhaps the accidents were attributed to the shape curve itself?

I drove back to the cemetery and entered the gates. When the road started to bend toward the back, I stopped and parked under some tall trees. *Guess this looks like a good vantage point of the place. Yes, I can see almost everything from here. So where shall we begin?*

I grabbed my camera and proceeded to explore. The cemetery was easy to walk because the graves were in rows. The majority of gravestones were in good condition. Many of them were large and shouted out the family names. There was William Ganong and his family members. As I read the inscriptions, I noticed different symbols on the stones. There were a lot of Masons buried there.

I paused for a moment to take it all in. My eyes glanced up the hill. Something seemed to be calling to me. Hey, what are you doing down there? We're all up here waiting for you. Hurry up already. Well, how could I resist that invitation? *Ok, I'll be right there just as soon as I figure out how to do that.* It looked rather steep, but manageable. It seemed an easy undertaking at first, but then half way up, my foot slipped into a crevice and I almost fell. *My, aren't we graceful? Is it any wonder that they don't get much company up here?* They were all most likely laughing at this blundering visitor. Slowly, I made my way to the top. The encounter was a little more menacing than expected. I couldn't believe how far up I had climbed. Going back down was going to be fun. Maybe I could just slide down.

As I walked around, I realized there was quite a contrast between the levels. It was almost as if I were in another world. The gravestones up there were very fragile and many of them had been vandalized. Some were broken in two and others were leaning up against trees. I could understand there being activity here. People must have been very upset about their markers being broken and their graves disturbed. And those leaning against the trees weren't anywhere near the proper resting spot of the person. It was very disheartening

I came upon a family plot consisting of a large gravestone and four small ones. I knelt down, pushed the grass aside and looked at the inscriptions. Much to my dismay, I had discovered four babies all leaving this world before the age of six months. As I touched each stone, I could feel the mother's sadness.

I moved along and then paused to read the inscriptions on two very old gravestones; a young husband and wife. *Wonder what caused them to die so young?* I thought I saw something out of the corner of my eye. To my right was a young couple standing next to a tall tree. They appeared to be in their twenties. I knew they weren't real because I could see through them, but I was sure they were watching me. The woman was wearing a long dress and the man was in a Confederate uniform. I turned and clicked my camera, but they were gone. Did these graves belong to them?

To my left was the sound of children giggling. I saw movement out of the corner of my eye again. There appeared to be two young boys standing by the fence wearing old fashioned clothes and caps. They were watching me, too. I turned and there was nothing. Were they playing hide and seek with me? I walked over to where they had been standing. There were graves that belonged to two children ages three and four. Then, my goodness, I got a vision of a ball rolling and a speeding train.

But before I could give it a second thought, there was another apparition standing by a tree. It was a young man wearing a Union uniform and holding a rifle. He looked at me, nodded and faded away behind the tree. *Ok, guys who's in charge around here? If you want to speak with me, you have to stand still a little longer.* As I looked down, there was a marker for Albert Ganong age 17 who had been a Union Soldier. How sad was that? Wonder what his story was all about?

Suddenly, I had an overpowering feeling that somebody was watching me again. *My gosh, everybody is so friendly here.* I looked around and at first saw nothing. Then I felt drawn to the back of the grounds. Further up the hill was a slender six foot gravestone. Beside the stone, stood a young woman. She was wearing a long white dress and had a ribbon in her short dark hair. *Oh my goodness. She does exist.*

Who was she? Why was she still there? I felt myself being guided to a broken gravestone lying on the round. *Is this you? Is this your grave?* I bent down and knelt on the ground. As I brushed the leaves away, I saw her name was Sarah Dickinson. She died in 1865 making her twenty years old. *How did you die, Sarah? Why are you still here?* Then I heard, "Help!" It sounded so desperate. I looked up, but now she was gone.

Most people would have run the opposite direction, but I ventured toward the back of the cemetery. After all this was the reason for being here. The further I went, the higher the incline. Was she hiding behind the gravestone? Maybe she was behind the big tree. I nervously peered around the corner. *Whatever you do, Sarah, please just don't jump out and scare me!* Fortunately or unfortunately, there was nobody there. I turned and my eyes panned the area. This was without a doubt the best vantage point in the cemetery. I could see everything from that spot. There was a perfect view of the entire grounds, the front gate and the road. Ok, so where was my woman in white?

My eyes scanned the grounds like finely tuned radar. If she was around, there would be no way of missing her. *Sarah, where are you? I'm here to help.* Soon I spied her standing near her grave. Slowing, I descended the hill keeping her in my sights. But before I reached the spot, she disappeared. This was so frustrating. I knew she was watching and wanted to communicate with me. Why did she keep walking away? Perhaps she wasn't sure she could trust me. What should I do? I wasn't giving up yet.

Over to the right was a stone bench. That would be perfect. I would sit down there and take out my recorder. Maybe I could coax her to come over and sit next to me. We could have a nice quiet conversation and not be interrupted. I hadn't seen the others around in awhile. My guess was they only wanted to show me their graves since no one seemed to remember them. Well, apparently I made the right decision coming here today.

I walked over to the bench and sat down. I was surprised at the temperature of the surface. It was eighty degrees out and yet the bench was cool. As I tried to get situated, I couldn't help but feel weird. It was as if I were sitting on somebody's gravestone. Was I supposed to be using this? Or was this placed here so that the residents might enjoy it? Hopefully I wasn't intruding.

I turned on the recorder and placed it on the bench. I moved all the way to the left leaving room for

Sarah. My eyes searched the surrounding area working their way to the top of the hill. There she was standing next to the tall gravestone again. *Sarah, can you please come down here and sit with me on the bench? I moved over so there would be enough room for your pretty dress.* I motioned to her to come. *You said you needed help. It's ok. Come sit with me and tell me what is wrong.* I watched for a moment and then she was gone.

A few seconds later, I felt a presence on my right side. I might have been crazy, but I swore I could feel the fabric of her long dress touching my leg as she sat down beside me. *Is that you Sarah? I'm so glad you decided to sit with me. Please tell me what's wrong.* At first, it was quiet. Then I heard her crying. "Where is he? He promised he'd come back. I've been looking and looking, but I can't find him." I felt her get up from the bench. "Help!" she cried and then she was gone.

I looked around the cemetery hoping to catch one more glimpse, but could not find her. I rewound the tape and listened. There it was loud and clear, "Help!" Who was this man she longed to find? Was it her husband? Why was there such a desperate sound in her voice? Quickly, I did some calculations in my head. My gosh, she's been searching for him almost148 years! No wonder she sounded desperate.

I walked back to her grave and looked at the marker once again. It said "Wife of Mathew S. Dickinson." I looked at the adjacent graves, but could not locate his. I took the notepad out of my pocket and recorded the information. I would go home and search the genealogy websites for more clues. Hopefully, I would discover something that would enable me to help her. *Good bye, Sarah. I have to go for now, but I'll be back soon. Promise.* As soon as the words passed my lips, I couldn't help but think that somebody else had spoken those exact words to her.

I couldn't wait to get back home. Would I be able to find out something about her? My fingers nervously typed her name in the search box. I wasn't expecting anything to show up, but there was always a slim chance. As soon as I hit the search key, both her and her husband appeared. I had not only discovered documentation; but there was an actual family tree. This was an incredible find. I clicked on the tree and low and behold, some photos were attached including one of Sarah and another of her husband. She looked exactly like the apparition that spoke to me. How was that for validation? I had taken several photos at the cemetery. Even though there were only glowing lights in them, I knew it was her.

The documents indicated they married on November 7, 1865. Sadly, she passed away December 8, 1865, only a month later. Could she be buried in her wedding dress? It didn't state a cause of death. I got a vision of her getting sick. It came on very sudden with chills and an excruciating headache. Then she fell asleep, but she never awoke. Unaware of her passing and possibly thinking she had just awakened from a deep sleep, Sarah continued to walk the lonely cemetery for many years in search of her beloved Mathew. Yes, she wandered for 148 years until I was able to communicate with her.

Mathew was a Union soldier during the Civil War. He was part of the 27th Regiment Michigan Infantry. His unit was known as the Sharp Shooters. Upon leaving for war, did Mathew promise to return and did Sarah promise to wait for him? Records show that after the war, he moved to California with his two sisters. That explained why there wasn't a grave. I followed his life and discovered he never remarried. Had he, at the age of 22, already decided his heart belonged only to his lovely Sarah? Was he waiting for her on the other side? I had to bring them back together.

There was also information about Albert Ganong. He was a Union soldier and part of the 24th Regiment Michigan Infantry. After being captured by the Confederates in December, he was sent to the notorious Libby Prison in Virginia. Conditions at the prison were deplorable. And with only bars on the windows, it made the elements his new enemy. Upon spending only a month there, he succumbed to pneumonia and his young life ended. Did he not know he gave his life for the cause? Did he think the war was still going on?

A few weeks later, I returned to the cemetery. *Sarah, I'm back. Where are you? I have something to tell you.* As I moved around the grounds, it felt eerily still. Nobody was watching me from behind the trees that day. Or so it seemed. I had brought some gifts for my new friends. There was a red rose for Sarah, a flag for the young man and a small teddy bear for the boys.

I walked to the fence and found the boy's graves. I placed the teddy bear on the ground. *Hi, I've got a teddy bear here. You can play with it if you want.* I took out my camera and snapped a few photos. Suddenly, the bear did a summersault. It startled me because the ground was flat and there was no wind that day. Reaching down, I returned him to his upright position. *Did somebody move this bear? Can you do it again?* Sure enough, teddy toppled head over heels once more. *Well, that was fun guys. Teddy is going to be right here so you can play with him whenever you want, ok?*

Next I walked over to the young man's grave and placed the flag in the ground. *Hope you like this. Every soldier needs to have one on their grave.* I looked up to find him standing by the tree once more. But just as before, he only nodded, perhaps this time in approval. Then he turned and vanished behind the tree.

I located Sarah's grave and laid the red rose on it. *Sarah, I brought you a pretty rose and put it on your grave. Do you like it?* I guess I was expecting a response, but got none. My eyes were drawn to the top of the hill. There she stood. Should I attempt to walk up there? Would she welcome me or run away like last time? Not wanting to engage in a game of hide and seek, I decided to stay where I was. Perhaps, I would sit on the stone bench again. I hoped she might join me there.

As I sat down on the bench, I looked back over my shoulder. She was no longer on the hill. *Please come sit next to me. Will you tell me how I can help?* I felt coldness on my right side. That was very strange considering it was eighty degrees. "When is he coming?" she whispered. "I've been waiting and waiting, but he's never there. He promised." Her voice sounded so sad. *Are you talking about Mathew?* "Yes, my Mathew, when is he coming?" she asked. I wasn't sure how to tell her that he wasn't coming. How could I get her to understand?

Sarah, listen to me. Mathew moved to California. He passed on a long time ago. He's not coming back. I heard a sigh. Then I felt her long dress brushing against my leg as if she were getting up. "No, he's coming back. He promised me. I love him so much," she whispered. "Help me!" Ok, I needed to try again. *Sarah, I know how much you miss him. But he can't come here. You need to go to him.* Hopefully she understood this time. "He told me to stay here and wait for him. He promised he would be back. Where is he?" she pleaded.

No matter what I said, she did not seem to comprehend the meaning of my words. Finally, feeling hopeless myself, I just blurted it out. *Sarah, Mathew is dead and so are YOU!* Immediately, I heard her cry out "Oh, no!" *Yes, you were very sick, fell asleep and never woke up.* All I could hear was sobbing. *Sarah, it's going to be all right. I'll show you how to get to Mathew. All you have to do is cross that beautiful bridge and go to the light. Do you see the bright light up ahead?*

She looked up, but hesitated. I felt her apprehension. She wanted to go, but wasn't sure it would be the right decision. After all, hadn't he told her to wait for him? Heaven help us now, Sarah. This was going to require some heavenly assistance.

Mathew, can you hear me? Sarah wants to come to you, but she's afraid. Can you please walk over to the bridge so she can see you? I looked across the bridge not certain if my message was being heard. After all, I was new at helping souls go to the light. But there he stood wearing his Union colors. He was so proud of that uniform. He had not aged one bit. Had he wanted to remain young so that they might continue where they left off?

Sarah, it's all right. Look on the other side of the bridge. I found him. It's Mathew! She turned slowly, faced the bridge and looked toward the light. It was so bright she had to squint. "Oh!" she exclaimed. Mathew reached out his arms. Without a second thought, she ran across the bridge and into his loving arms again. "You came back for me just like you promised!" she cried. I watched as they embraced. He was so elated to see her that he lifted her feet off the ground just like in the old movies. "Mathew, I love you so much! she gushed. She helped me find you! I knew you would come back!"

William Ganong Cemetery, Westland, MI

Sarah Ann Dickinson

Light anomaly by the tree

Light anomaly on top of the hill where Sarah stands

"Relax," said the night man,
"We are programmed to receive
You can check out any time you like,
But you can never leave."

--- Eagles

Chapter 15

Ohio State Reformatory

Dusk was approaching and the fog was rolling in. The cry of a lonesome train whistle filled the night air. I drove along the winding path known as Reformatory Road. Up ahead, a huge Gothic structure stood vigilant in the mist. Its presence was like no other and it was as though the building somehow commanded my attention. I found myself unable to escape the clutches of the mysterious forces already taking hold of me. This imposing monument was known as Ohio State Reformatory. I gasped at its spectacular beauty which defied the imagination. I could feel the rhythm of her heartbeat as if she were somehow alive.

The sprawling grounds were at one time used as a Civil War training area. Camp Mordecai Bartley, named after the governor, was the first stop for many young Union soldiers. However, many of them did not make it to the battle fields before succumbing to other adversaries such as measles, small pox and diphtheria.

After the war ended, the state commissioned Levi T. Scofield to design the structure. He created it in a cathedral-like image in hopes of encouraging inmates to experience a spiritual rebirth and turn their lives around for the better. In 1896, it opened its doors to 150 young offenders. The premise was to reform first timers by offering them school and teaching them a new trade.

The institution was supposed to be a halfway point between the Boys Industrial School and the State Penitentiary. Many inmates were actually rehabilitated and reintroduced back into society where they lived full and productive lives. However, as time passed, more and more repeat offenders returned to the institution. Overcrowding and violence eventually produced unbearable conditions causing the federal government to shut them down. By the time the reformatory closed its doors, it had housed over 155,000 men.

The majestic facility was in the process of being demolished when the Mansfield Reformatory Preservation Society stepped in to save it. It is now listed in the National Register of Historic Places as one of the five largest castle-like structures in the United States. The East Cell Block is the largest steel free-standing cell block in the world at six tiers high.

The last inmates were released from the prison in 1990. Or were they? Many restless spirits of prisoners, workers and guards are said to have remained. Why is that? Are they unable to escape the prison's bars even though the cell doors are unlocked? Are they unaware that they are deceased? Perhaps they remain because moving on would mean being banished forever to the fires of hell. I had to find out.

In order to fund the restoration of the building, tours are conducted. Likewise, at times, a lucky few are allowed overnight investigations. That night I was part of a group that would be spending the night. Would we encounter any of the lost souls? Hopefully we would be able to communicate with them and discover the story they had waited so long to tell.

A long driveway lead up to the front entrance where I was greeted by the honking of the Canadian geese welcoming committee. As the gates closed behind me, the clanging sound of metal reminded me this was the real thing. Suddenly, that song came to mind, "You can check out any time you like, but you can never leave." What would I discover behind those walls which were designed to restrain men from the freedom they longed to own once again?

When I arrived at the prison, I met up with Ken and Russ. We sat on the front steps a few minutes taking it all in and admiring her glory. Let's face it, we were thunder-struck. There were no words to accurately describe this amazing place. "Wow," seemed so inadequate yet fitting.

We put our heads together and began to devise a plan for the evening. What would be our first stop? What equipment should we use? Hopefully there were enough batteries. And most importantly, did anybody have to go to the bathroom? Silly as it sounded, once the mission had begun, there would be no time for such trivial distractions. The guys said they wanted to keep me from harm's way that night. One of them would walk ahead of me and the other behind. It was comforting to know chivalry and gallantry were qualities of my fellow investigators.

After ascending the most spectacular wooden staircase, we began our investigation in the Warden's quarters. This was where he and the assistant warden once resided with their families. The rooms, each adorned with a beautiful fireplace, had been decorated with Victorian style accents. It must have been a grand sight to see in its day. Of course, it was difficult to imagine raising children in such a place. Although it wasn't your average neighborhood, they obviously considered it home. I wondered if that old saying, "Wait until your father gets home." Had any special meaning to children living near a prison.

A small stage stood at the back of the room. Twinkling stars peeked through the window awaiting the next performance. What type of entertainment did they enjoy? Wouldn't it be great to catch a lingering melody? Perhaps, if we listened very carefully, we might hear a few cords of the waltz that played as couples gracefully floated about the dance floor.

We decided to sit there and attempt to communicate with any family members who might be in the area. I set the K-II Meter on the floor.

Hello, I hope we aren't intruding. Sorry but we let ourselves in. I just want you to know you have a very lovely place here. Since it is Friday night, we were wondering if there was anything special going on. If you would be so kind as to join us, we would love some company. I just put a little box on the floor. It has a green light. Would it be possible for you to light up the other lights so we know you are here?

Suddenly, to the right there was the sound of footsteps walking on the wooden floor. The lights on the meter flashed. Before we could acknowledge our visitor, a black shadow figure walked across the room and entered another. Obviously, the person was not interested in joining us. Russ hurried over to the room hoping to catch a glimpse of our elusive visitor, but he had vanished.

Thank you for letting your presence be known. It's ok if you don't wish to join us tonight. Is there anybody else here that would like to communicate with us?

From where we were seated on the stage, there was a great view of the stairs. It was then that the shadow figure of a woman wearing a long dress appeared. She walked from the right staircase across the landing and up the left staircase. I hurried over to the stairs and looked up, but she was gone. I decided to stay near the stairs in hopes of catching a glimpse of her again.

Having three sides of the room covered, we proceeded to call upon anyone else who had ventured into the room. My eyes were fixed to the top of the stairs. Ken manned the K-II meter. He invited anyone there to approach him. The lights on the meter lit up from green to red.

At that same moment, I saw movement on the left side of the stairs. There were two small boys, perhaps eight years of age, poking their heads over the railing. One boy had dark hair and the other was blond. They possibly had on their Sunday best as they were wearing long sleeve shirts and dark pants. Maybe they were curious about how our K-II worked. But just as quickly, they crouched down behind the rail.

Did the person that lit up the lights live here at one time? Is there anyone else among us that lived here? Please respond by walking up to our machine and lighting the lights.

The lights on the meter flashed. I heard the sound of giggling coming from the top of the stairs. The two boys were leaning over the rail looking down toward the lights. Then they quickly crouched back down behind the railing possibly thinking I couldn't see them there.

How many people are visiting with us tonight? When we say the correct number, will somebody please let us know by lighting up the lights? Are there two? Maybe three? Or is it four?

At four, the lights on the meter flashed again. Our young friends must have found it all so amusing as they began to giggle once more. They really did think they could not be seen hiding behind the railing.

Well, thank you so much for inviting us into your home tonight. It's getting late and we don't want to wear out our welcome. Besides I think it is way past bed time for little boys. Good night guys.

Gentle fingers of light from the full moon reached in from outside guiding our way as we headed over to the East Cell Block. To our left, six tiers of rusted cells towered over us. It was a humbling experience. The paint that had once covered the walls and cold iron bars had long since begun to chip, peel and curl. And yet, despite their decaying appearance, they continued to maintain their dignity. If these walls could talk, would they share the secrets they harbor? Or would they forever hold within them the thoughts of men who had not been able to shake free from their daunting memories. It seemed these were the walls of lost hopes and dreams.

I entered one of the cells and sat down on the rusted remains of the small metal frame. There appeared to be some sort of writing on the crumbling wall. Was this a warning to others from someone who had entered this place long ago? Or was it the crazed scribbling of a man who had gone mad after being held captive in his own mind? What horror came over him as he was unable to escape those thoughts of regret: woulda, shoulda, coulda? Had he realized this knowing would forever be haunting deep within the annals of his mind and no amount of penance could erase it?

Or maybe it was a deranged psychopath who did not possess any morals or pangs of conscience. Had he absolutely no remorse for his dastardly deeds and no qualms about committing some more? Perhaps he sat in the darkness contemplating his next heinous crime or calculating a means of escaping these walls. Nevertheless, I could feel the stifling energy afflicted with despair as it surrounded me. It was like a story with no ending or a verse without a rhyme. It longed for completion that would never come.

After leaving the cell, we noticed a bench in the corner and decided to sit there awhile and conduct an EVP session. We were all eager to see the Spirit Box in action. I turned it on while Ken held the recorder in his hand. Hopefully, we would get lucky and pick up some good responses to our questions. Lucky indeed.

Is there anyone here that would like to speak with us? I have a black box in my hand that will enable you to communicate. Immediately, we heard, "Steve."

Hi, Steve why are you here?

"Stole some money."

How much money did you steal?

"Enough."

Oh, lucky you. I guess you got away with enough money to live the good life.

"It wasn't that much."

How old are you, Steve?

"Twenty."

How long have you been here?

"Long time."

Thank you, Steve. How many more people are here with us
tonight? Can somebody please tell us?

"Four"

Who else is here? Can you tell us your name?

"Russ."

Hi, Russ why are you here?

"Duh, I died!"

Well, ok, I guess we figured that much. Did you get caught
stealing something like Steve?

"No."

Then what did you do?

"Killed my wife."

Oh, my goodness, what was her name?

"Jo"

Is there anybody else here?

"Tom."

Hi, Tom, why are you here?

"Beat him up."

Why did you do that?

"Because!"

Is anyone else here?

"Willie, the big one."

Hi, Willie, why are you here?

"Killed a woman."

Oh, why did you do that?

"Caught her with that guy."

Is there anyone else here that wants to speak? You said there were four with us.

"Isaac ."

Hi, Isaac, why are you here?

"Can't say."

Speak up now. Don't be shy. You're among friends. We promise we won't hurt you.

"No."

Ok, then tell us how the food is in here.

"It's all right."

When was the last time you had a cold beer?

"Long time."

What do you guys do for fun in here? Do you play craps?

"We do."

Can you tell us what day it is?

"Friday."

Good, can you tell us what month it is?

"June."

It appeared we were having quite an interaction with the inmates. They were more than eager to share their stories with us. We decided to try another strategy. Ken leaned over and placed the K-II Meter on the floor.

Ken just put a little box on the floor. It has a green light. Can somebody light up the other lights? You've probably had people ask you that before.
"Oh, ya."

Within seconds, the entire sequence of lights lit up from green to red. Apparently, the spirits in our presence were well-versed in paranormal equipment.

That was great. If you are one of the people we were just talking with, can you please light up the lights? Again, the lights responded.

If you are standing next to me, can you touch my arm? Suddenly, the area to my left became very cool. I felt fingers lightly stroke my arm. The hair on my arm was standing up because of the electrical energy. My other arm felt normal. *Wow, just think, I was being touched by an inmate.* That was creepy. And I didn't know which one was touching me. Was it the thief or the murderer? That was doubly creepy.

Thank you. Now can you walk over to the guys? Immediately, I felt the cool spot dissipate. And right on cue, both guys felt the coolness in front of them.

Thank you. That was very good. You're probably getting tired of us. If you want us to leave, can you please light up the lights again?

Without hesitation, all the lights lit up. *Well, thank you for sharing your stories with us. We really appreciate it. Guess that means we will be moving on like we promised. It was great talking with you.*

Since we wanted to be good guests, it seemed only fitting to keep our word and move on. The spirits had graciously allowed us their time and hopefully we would cross paths again some day. We packed up our gear and started walking toward the stairs. But before we got very far we heard the distinct clanking sound of a cell door closing. Had one of our new friends turned in for the night?

Russ quickly took a few quick photos toward the direction of the sound in hopes of identifying our elusive friend. I also snapped off several more shots with the full spectrum camera. This is able to capture the entire range of the light spectrum from ultraviolet (UV) light to infrared (IR) light. Natural lighting is full spectrum, but we are not capable of seeing UV light above the spectrum or IR light below the spectrum with the naked eye. It is thought that spirits can only be seen within these two extreme ranges. This is why we sometimes see entities out of the corner of our eye or not at all.

Upon review, Russ was disappointed to have not secured the likeness of our now quiet inmate. Before I even looked through mine, I had already convinced myself that I was not successful either. However, much to my amazement, there was a strange light mass in one of the photos. It appeared as if something was attempting to manifest. *Wow!* This anomaly was not present in the photo before or after. *Thank you once again for making your presence known. And as we promised, we'll be moving on.*

We started to descend the stairs in search of the infamous Solitary Confinement or as they loving referred to it, the Hole. Russ led the way followed by me and my shadow, Ken. I felt the pressure of a hand on my shoulder holding me back for a moment. I turned and asked Ken why he grabbed my shoulder. He assured me it wasn't him. Was it somebody who still had something else to say? Or was it somebody that didn't want me to speak with a spirit in the basement? But before we took another step, Russ said, "Look!" Down near the end of the hall in the shadows were what appeared to be a set of eyes; red eyes! Quickly we came to the consensus that somebody had been trying to warn me to get the heck out of there. We didn't waste one more second deciding what to do.

As soon as we reached Solitary, the air became very heavy. An unsettling darkness seemed to envelop the halls. The negative energy was so thick one could cut it with a knife. *Oops, sorry about the cutting with a knife stuff! Didn't mean to offend anyone.*

Solitary was reserved for those prisoners who committed an offense inside the prison. It was presumed that by isolating a man and his thoughts from the general population, it would bring him closer to the Creator. As he sat and contemplated his actions, he might learn to repent. Unfortunately, very seldom was this the case.

The Solitary cell did not have bars. Instead, there was a metal door with only a small slot in it. These men were not afforded the luxury of knowing the passage of time. Without any windows acknowledging the existence of the sun rising and setting, the men were at the mercy of their own minds. Had it been five minutes or five hours? They couldn't be sure. The only two constants were the deafening silence and the unbearable loneliness.

What effect would the loneliness have on a man? Would he experience it to such a degree that he felt the walls closing in on him? Would it become so intense and overpowering that it felt as if a hand were squeezing his heart? Or would it escalate to the point of sheer delirium as was the case of the man who set himself on fire?

As we slowly walked the narrow corridor, many questions came to mind. Who might we encounter in these halls? Would it be somebody that possessed enough fortitude to withstand their self-inflected mental torture? Would it be men who finally succumbed to the demons within themselves? Or would it be a part of their personality that had somehow separated only to remain inside the belly of the beast that had devoured them?

I entered a cell and sat down on the metal frame that used to be the only comfort a prisoner would know. A gruff man came forward. He projected himself as a person who could withstand anything the guards would throw his way. That being said, he decided to display his almighty attitude one day and start a fight with one of them. As his punishment, he was sent to Solitary Confinement.

After enduring days and days of what he considered boredom, he found himself reliving what had transpired. The story wreaked havoc as it played over and over in his mind. He remembered the adrenaline pulsing through his body like a freight train out of control. The sound of the bullets taking flight reverberated in his ears as the butt of the rifle recoiled against his shoulder. A faint wisp of smoke floated up from its angry metal mouth. The clink of the shell casings hitting the floor brought him back to reality.

He felt satisfaction in knowing his competition had been eliminated. But only hours later, the horror was returned to him two-fold. His wife had taken rat poison because she could not bear to live without her lover.

Many nights he lay on the cold damp cell floor curled up in a fetal position. Sometimes he would rock back and forth for what seemed like hours. He gripped his shaking fingers around his head crying out for some forgiveness. But nothing came. He longed to tell his mother he would do any penance if only she would hold him one more time. But that never happened.

My heart ached with his pain and I knew at last he was sincere. He told me his name was Herman Beckham. *Thank you so much for sharing your story. But why do you remain here?*

"I know now that no matter how much I pour out my heart to my wife, she will never forgive me or look at me again. I don't deserve to be loved," he said. "This is where I belong."

As we passed into the West Cell Block, we detected the unwavering beams of moonlight silently piercing through the darkness like bayonets. With shards of glass crunching beneath my feet, I neared the remnants of what once was a window. The big orb in the night sky resembled a disembodied soul. For an instant, it almost appeared to have a face; one with dark haunting eyes. Was she our constant companion this evening or a stalker in the darkness?

We entered the shower room, walked all the way back and sat down on a long bench. Since the Spirit Box proved to be so successful on the East Block, it was only fitting that the spirits on the West Block should have a stab at it. *Oops! There I go again. It was just a figure of speech guys.*

What kind of spirits would frequent a shower room? The stillness was overpowering. Its silent emptiness spoke of secrets. The all encompassing darkness hovered around us. I switched on the Sprit Box and Ken held the K-II Meter. Rumor had it that a man named Mr. Anderson would frequent the area. There were also some other baseball fanatics that enjoyed discussing the box scores. Perhaps we would be lucky enough to hear their opinion of the game.

Hey guys, I've got some baseball box scores here if anyone is interested. You don't mind talking shop with a woman, do you? Mr. Anderson, are you with us tonight? If you are, could you please approach the green light on the box?

With no response from either device, I proceeded to call out the scores. *Mr. Anderson, it looks like your favorite team is doing well this week. According to the newspaper the Dodgers shut out the Pirates 3-0. What do you think about that?*

Immediately, the lights on the K-II went from green to red.

Is that you Mr. Anderson? If it is, can you please do it one more time? Without hesitation the lights flashed again.

Thank you, Mr. Anderson. Did you bring any other sports fans with you tonight? Is there anybody here that likes the Pirates?

"I do!"

Well, that's great. Let's check out how they're doing this week. Pirates 5, Cincinnati 4 … Pirates 4, Cincinnati 0 … Hey that sounds good. What do you think?

"Ya!"

Oh no, looks like an upset, Tigers 6, Pirates 5. What do you think about that?

"It stinks!"

If you get out soon, maybe you can go to a Pirates game and cheer them on. It has probably been a long time. What do you think?
"Great!"

Who am I speaking with? Can you tell me your name?

"Robert"

Can you tell me why you're here?

"Got caught!"

Do you have anything else to say?

"I do." ….. "Sorry."

Do you know Steve?

"Ya."

How many people are with us tonight?

"Four"

Can you please come forward and tell me your name?

"Freeman"

Do you have a message for us?

"We're in trouble!"

Suddenly, there was a loud bang near the door. It sounded as though something had been thrown. Russ jumped up and looked out into the hall. There was nobody there and he couldn't find anything lying around. Had somebody new entered the room? What did Freeman mean about being in trouble?

We just heard that bang. Is there somebody new in the room? Can you please respond by approaching the green light?

Without hesitation, our visitor flashed the lights. I noticed the energy around me began to feel lighter. Then much to my surprise, I felt a hand gently touch my elbow.

Who are you? Are you an inmate? There was no response. *Are you a guard?* The lights on the meter flashed.

Well, no wonder the others made a bee line for the door. The guard was most likely doing his rounds checking for any foolery going on. But why was he still there? There would be no proverbial chains to bind him as were the case with the inmates.

I asked him if he could come forward and speak to me. Did he die here? Was he involved in some sort of scuffle with a prisoner? The man said his name was Thomas. He didn't mean to startle me when he touched my elbow. No, he didn't die at the prison. He was happily married to a lovely woman who blessed him with three children. It was such a privilege being part of the prison that he wanted to come back again. With that he tipped his hat, nodded his head and bid me farewell. On that note, we decided to call an end to our investigation. We knew everything was in good hands as long as Thomas was around. *Good night everyone. It was a pleasure meeting you. I know we'll be back real soon.*

Ohio State Reformatory, Mansfield, OH

Spirit trying to manifest

"Well, the towns lay out across the dusty plains
Like graveyards filled with tombstones,
Waitin' for the names."

--- Eagles

Chapter 16

Tombstone

As we approached the forsaken desert town, a lone tumbleweed, an easy prey for the wind, turned end over end across the plains. The sun stood high and righteous in the afternoon sky. How many gunfights at high noon was he privy to? How many hangings did he officiate at as he looked out over the gallows at day break? Surely he had enough memories to write quite a few dime novels. But alas, he was keeping his cards close to his vest like a gambler in a high stakes poker game.

As we drove on, the desolate road rose up to meet us; yet two more drifters merely passing through. I looked over at my friend Jesse and remarked, "We should be coming up on the ranch with the fence made out of antlers." He gave me a rather puzzled look and said, "What are you talking about? We've never been here before."

"Ya, we have," I insisted. "How could you have forgotten something so cool?" He shook his head and said, "I have no idea what you're talking about. You must be thinking about some other place. I'm telling you, we've never been this way before." Not wanting to engage in a debate of epic proportion, I ceased talking about it. But I know when I'm right.

A few minutes later, hundreds of antlers intertwined with great precision spread out before our eyes. It was just as I remembered. "See. There it is," I exclaimed as my finger waved in the air like a teacher's pointer. "Do you remember it now?"

"No, because we've never been here before," he said. Now feeling a bit frustrated, I felt the need to make a point. "Then how was I able to describe it and tell you where it was?" He just shrugged his shoulders. *Yes, how was it you were able to describe something in such detail that you've never seen before? That was very weird.*

Come to think of it, I had been having a number of weird experiences the past few days. Two days ago we had stopped in Boulder, Colorado for the night. We saw the most magnificent hotel and without question had to spend the night. The five story Boulderado Hotel was built in 1909. It was thought that a name comprised of a clever combination of Boulder and Colorado would leave a lasting impression in the minds of its many visitors. With the imposing peaks of the Rocky Mountains in the background, it looked like a beautiful picture postcard. The Victorian style structure with its stained glass ceiling was absolutely spectacular. Although the thought of ascending the amazing cherry wood staircase extending to the fifth floor seemed tempting to us, we chose to ride the original 1908 Otis elevator and were accompanied by our very own elevator attendant.

We stepped off the elevator and turned down the hallway toward our rooms. Up ahead was room 304. Upon opening the door, I swore it felt as if somebody rushed past me, but I dismissed it as my imagination. After all I was exhausted having traveled so many miles that day. What I needed now was a goodnight's sleep so I could enjoy Colorado tomorrow. I was especially looking forward to taking a stroll down Pearl Street.

The east and west bound streets of the area were closed to traffic and it was converted into an outdoor mall. Pearl Street Mall was a unique place. Although best known as the backdrop for Mork and Mindy of TV fame, it was also famous for its eclectic array of sidewalk entertainers. Artists would set up their easels and for a few dollars paint your portrait. Musicians sang as those passing by tossed coins into the guitar case sitting on the sidewalk. On the other side of the spectrum were nimble-fingered jugglers and tightrope walkers performing death-defying feats on the wire they had suspended between the lamp posts. And of course, there were mimes pretending to find their way out of that invisible box. All in all it proved to be an interesting place.

With that said I climbed into bed and snuggled up with my pillow. A few seconds after closing my eyes, I was startled to hear footsteps. It sounded like somebody had walked across the room. I sprang up in bed and my eyes scanned the room for an intruder, but there was nobody there. Did I really hear something or was I only dreaming? I couldn't be sure. Without giving it a second thought, I lay back down. *Just relax and enjoy this wonderful bed.*

But oh no, we couldn't do that. A few seconds later, I felt the sensation of somebody sitting down at the foot of the bed. *Yikes!* Being positively certain I was not dreaming at that point, I was afraid to open my eyes. *Oh, but you must!* And I was determined to put this to rest so that I might get some much needed sleep.

I cautiously looked over my shoulder and caught a glimpse of an indentation on the mattress that was slowly deepening. *Hello, this is really happening!* My mind became inundated with all sorts of images as I moved with great speed to secure the covers over my head. *Now what?* Gripping my pillow tight as if it was going to somehow protect me and like a cat sizing up its prey, I ever so slowly attempted to peek from under the covers only to see nothing there. *Really?*

Undoubtedly, this was not my imagination. Now I found myself entertaining the idea that even though I stipulated my wanting a single room, I was not the only guest here. *Ok, who do I have the honor of meeting tonight? Please come out where I can see you.*

The air around me started to get cool. Then at last I saw my mysterious friend standing at the foot of the bed. He appeared to be so forlorn. I could feel the overwhelming sadness in his heart as he related his story to me.

In 1924, a couple spent the night in room 304. With big child-like eyes, they gazed out the window captivated by the beautiful snow capped peaks. The man leaned in, gently kissed his wife, the only good thing in his life, on the forehead and stretched his arm around giving her a big hug.

"This is such a romantic setting, isn't it, dear? she said. He just smiled. "Hope this little holiday makes you feel better." She gently squeezed his hand and then excused herself as she retreated into the bathroom for a warm bath.

The man sat quietly on the edge of the bed and stared out the window. This time however, his thoughts were somewhere else entirely. He began to think about everything and nothing. Where had he gone so wrong? Why did he experience such a disconnection with the rest of the world? What was the point of living?

Calmly he reached into his suitcase and pulled out a bottle of chloroform that had been secretly tucked away beneath his neatly folded clothes. Not being able to bear one more minute of life's tribulations, he applied a generous amount to the cloth, held it over his nose and deeply breathed in his last pitiful breath. At last he was able to successfully accomplish something.

Upon returning from the bathroom, the woman found her husband lying on the bed with his arm hanging over the side. On the floor was the cloth laced with the noxious fluid which had fallen from his now lifeless hand.

Her worst fears had been imagined as she realized her husband had committed suicide. A gambit of emotions pulsed through her numb body. Why did she leave him alone? Why did she not notice any warning signs? What would she do now? How would she ever go on without him?

Her heart ached and she was so terribly distraught. Perhaps the cloudiness of her vision caused her to reach a hasty decision. In her mind she knew there was only one thing to do. Hoping to once again be with her husband and rewrite the last words she said to him, she reached for the cloth and attempted to join him. But alas, there had not been enough chloroform remaining to fulfill her wish.

My mysterious roommate looked over at me with sadness in his eyes. Although he had experienced a feeling of accomplishment and satisfaction through his last actions, he had come to realize that he had instead failed miserably again. The only solace he had was when his wife had eventually forgiven him because she felt he did not know what he was doing.

I looked at the shattered man who continued to hold on to the place where he and his loving wife shared their last kiss. *It was nice meeting you. Thank you so much for sharing your story. I feel honored to know such a wonderful man. I want you to remember that you really are special. I'm sure if you go to the light, your wife will be waiting with open arms.*

Then he was gone. A calmness filled the air as if he understood. I snuggled up with my pillow once again and pulled up the covers. *Good night.*

The next morning when we checked out, the desk clerk asked, "Did you enjoy your stay with us? Did you sleep well last night?" *Oh, yes I slept like a baby; a baby that was terrified of the creepy clown staring at them that somebody had put into the crib. Slept like a baby that quietly whimpered as their eyes followed the eerie shapes moving about on the ceiling from the cute little motion night light. Yes, I slept just fine after all the shenanigans in my room finally ceased. Thank you very much.* But I retained my composure and politely said, "Yes, I did."

The clerk obviously noticed the look of distain on my face and perhaps a hint of sarcasm in my voice. It was then when I detected a smirk that he was trying to hold back. I asked him why he was smiling and this time he gave me a sheepish grin. He matter-of-factly said, "Well, you do know that room has spirits, don't you?" *Wow, thanks for sharing. It would have been nice to be privy to this information last night.* "Well, I did not," I replied. "However, after last night it was apparent I wasn't entirely alone."

"So you had the pleasure of meeting one of our special guests," he said. "Congratulations. Everyone is not so blessed." I wasn't sure that blessed was the most accurate word to describe my experience, but it was unforgettable.

Jesse was somewhat disappointed having had an uneventful night. But it was now time to set our sights on new adventures. At the moment, we were both excited to reach our new destination. We had been hoping to investigate here for a long time.

Up ahead we saw the sign: Tombstone; a ghost of a town. Here in the lawless Old West many a man came to seek their fortune. Some however, embraced the less honest way and died in a blaze of glory.

In 1877, Edward Schieffelin was a U.S. Calvary Scout at Fort Hauchuca in the Arizona Territory. He was also a prospector that enjoyed spending his spare time searching for valuable ore samples. The fort was located in the valley by the San Pedro River surrounded mostly by rattlesnakes, gila monsters, bands of Apaches and Cochise. It was a very dangerous area especially for somebody going out on their own as he often did. His friend Al Sieber warned him, "The only rock you will find out there will be your own tombstone."

He continued to search until he was almost out of money. Then just when he thought his luck had run out, he discovered a rich vein of silver on a plateau called Goose Flats. On September 21, 1877, he filed his claim and proudly named it Tombstone. Others hearing about the riches to be found laid their stakes on adjacent land and filed their own claims. As he and his brother set about mining, homesteaders and business men moved west and established a town nearby. They adopted the name Tombstone for their new home. It became the fastest growing town between St. Louis and San Francisco complete with stores, theaters, a school, church and over 100 saloons. The town was divided into two sections; for some it was a life of luxury while for others it was a life that was hard and fast.

Despite all the rich history of the town, it seems most people remember it for the infamous gunfight at the O.K. Corral (Old Kindersley). However, in all actuality, the conflict took place on Fremont Street on a narrow lot adjacent to Fly's Boarding House and Photographic Studio which was six doors west of the rear entrance to the O.K. Corral.

At 3:00 p.m. on October 26, 1881, an argument that later turned into ugly threats unfolded into a shoot out. Tom and Frank McLaury, Ike and Billy Clanton and Bill Claiborne stared down lawmen Wyatt, Virgil and Morgan Earp and Doc Holiday. The opposing sides initially only six feet apart exchanged gunfire lasting all of sixty seconds. Three outlaws Tom, Frank and Billy were sent to Boot Hill that day. For Billy Clanton it was his first gunfight and his last. It is said that their spirits still walk the streets.

There are also twenty-six other documented spirits that wander the buildings perhaps having no knowledge of their demise. Do they long to roll the dice one more time or engage in a game of faro or high stakes poker? Perhaps they wish to down a few more beers while enjoying the show girls on stage. Whatever the reason, they continue to live on so to speak in the town too tough to die.

And that was why we were there. Hopefully, we would be able to connect with some of these spirits, learn their stories and get a feel for the Wild West. As we parked the truck, we tried to decide where to explore first. We both agreed the Bird Cage would be the most interesting place to begin. Little did I know how interesting it would turn out to be.

As soon as I stepped out of the truck, a strange sensation came over me. My head was spinning and my legs were unsteady. It was almost as though I was floating in space. I swore it felt as if I had just walked through some type of portal. Although I was fully aware of my surroundings, there was a part of me that was immerging into another dimension.

Then all of a sudden I blurted out, "There is a long bar on the left side of the room. The wall behind it has a huge mirror. On the right side are tables where they used to play cards and stairs leading to the floor above. The stage is all the way to the back of the room. I used to sing up there." *Wait a minute. You used to sing up there?*

I looked over at Jesse who was now giving me the strangest look. "What the heck are you mumbling about now?" Once again he was just shaking his head at my babbling. "Let's get going inside."

I was still feeling a bit unbalanced, but managed to start walking over to the building. And unbalanced was an understatement. I felt as if I had been imbibing in several shots of Red Eye. Whoa, what just happened there? I had never experienced anything of that sort before. It just didn't make sense to me.

The sound of our footsteps on the wooden walkway rang in my ears. Clomp. Clomp. It sounded eerily familiar, but how could that be? Jesse opened the door and stepped inside. He didn't get very far before he stopped right in his tracks. He turned around and looked at me dumbfounded. "How did you know this?" he asked. "Well, I've been here many times. I took the train," I said. *Train? Now you rode the train?*

I began to lose my balance and it felt as though my soul was attempting to ascend from my body. Somehow, I made my way over to a chair, sat down and hung on for dear life. But suddenly I felt myself being whisked away to another time.

The New Mexico-Arizona train slowly pulled into the station. As the brakes locked, the wheels screeched to a stop sending sparks over the rails. I began to step off and a cloud of steam rose up and surrounded me. Carefully, I gathered up my long skirt so as not to get tangled around my high buttoned shoes during my decent.

My gentleman companion took my hand and assisted me off the last step and onto the platform.

The pungent smell of oil from the hanging lantern permeated deep into my sinuses. The lantern had been hung on the hook in order to signal the oncoming train of passengers waiting to board. From here, my two companions and I would board the stagecoach for the next nine miles headed for Tombstone. There we would entertain the town folk with our songs. We were traveling troubadours that complemented each other well and were welcomed everywhere we went. Afterward, we were on to the next town for another performance.

The stagecoach was my least favorite part of the trip. The ride was often bumpy, dusty and hot. And there was always the fear of desperados lurking in the eves. So far we had been graced with the good fortune of escaping such travesties.

Upon arriving in town, we hurried to the hotel to find our rooms. We had barely enough time to brush off the dust and freshen up a bit. I changed my dress from something comfortable to one more glamorous and adjusted the hair pins holding my long hair atop my head.

Quickly we found our way back stage. I could hear the low murmuring of the audience as they patiently waited for the show to begin. The piano player tapped his foot in time as his fingers danced over the ebony and ivory keys. The curtains on the stage opened and we broke into song. Applause, applause …

"Hello, earth calling," said Jesse as he shook my arm. "Where did you wander off?" Well, I wasn't exactly certain, but I was sure glad he pulled me back from where ever it was. Had I just experienced a Past Life? I had heard of such things, but never actually believed in them. However, there was no mistaking what had happened. I had felt my body being pulled into another dimension. Only after my arm was tugged, did it render me back to reality.

But what was reality? For a moment, it was difficult to distinguish between this and the other plane because I felt equally existent in both. My hand reached up to touch my hair expecting to feel those hair pins. But instead, my long tresses rested on my shoulders. I looked down and was no longer wearing period clothing. Back were my Boulder Colorado t-shirt and jeans. *Better keep this day dream to yourself. Nobody will ever believe you. They'll probably think you were out in the desert sun too long.*

Then I heard the sound of cards being shuffled and the clink of poker chips being dropped on the table next to me. "Tell me you heard that," I said. "Please don't let me be the only one enjoying all this."

"Ya, I heard something," he said. "What was that?" I felt relieved that somebody else was finally having a personal experience. We were actually hearing sounds without the use of a recorder.

"Sounds to me like they're playing cards and dropping chips on the table," I replied. Jesse agreed. Suddenly, we both jumped as we heard the clinking of glass behind the bar. The faint smell of whiskey and stale cigar smoke lingered in the air. Then we spun around as a lone C-sharp came from the piano at the far end of the room. Was the place coming alive or was it only residual energy? We couldn't be sure, but just the same it was amazing.

Just in case our encounter had been real, we thanked the spirits before moving on. Then we stepped back outside and walked down the street to the O.K. Corral hoping to interact with anyone that might be there.

I had to admit I was slightly disenchanted when finally laying eyes on the infamous corral. Perhaps there was an unrealistic expectation of becoming one with a moment in history and feeling the intense energy. Instead, there we were in a huge empty space between the buildings staring at some old hitching posts. No wonder the Old West writers embellished the story a bit. There did not appear to be much happening here.

Suddenly, a figure moved across the corral and walked right through the wall. It was a man wearing a long black frock coat and cowboy hat. Then we heard a woman giggling over by the horse stalls. Upon investigating I saw a vision of a cowboy and a saloon girl rolling around in the hay. As they kissed, he threw his hat into the corner. She had pieces of hay stuck in her hair and her long skirt was hiked up above the knees exposing her black lace stockings. *Oh my goodness! Time to move along!*

We walked out into Freemont Street imagining how it must have felt that day. I wondered what other gunfights may have occurred here. Undoubtedly, the energy must have been ominous and electrifying. I began to feel a strange sensation and decided it best to kneel down a moment. In my mind's eye, I saw a vision from long ago.

Rage pulsed through his veins like a charging bull and the blood vessels in his temples throbbed like big base drums. His eyes saw red as he felt an insurmountable animosity for the lawman trying to dictate whether or not he had a right to carry a gun. He refused to back down like a scared dog cowering to his abusive master. That last shot of courage at the saloon ignited a fury that invoked a righteous confidence and undeniable fierceness. He felt a justified entitlement and was going to act upon it.

He called out to the lawman and challenged him. As the marshal stood there, the sun illuminating the gold star on his chest, he knew he had no other choice, but to stand his ground against the mockery and relentless disrespect displayed by the man.

Two shots rang out and the sound reverberated in the air. Moments later, a wisp of black smoke floated from the barrel of the Colt 45. Only one man remained standing. The other laying motionless in the dirt his cold dead hand still gripping the gun he refused to surrender. Soon he would join the forgotten at Boot Hill.

Boot Hill Cemetery, Tombstone, AZ

Bird Cage Theatre

O.K. Corral

"Long may you run,
Although these changes have come.
With your chrome heart shining
In the sun
Long may you run."

--- Neil Young

Chapter 17

Hell

Just off US-23 the road meandered vicariously through the tranquil countryside. A mother duck and her ducklings waddled by on their way to the lake. The soothing rays of the afternoon sun made the idea of a swim quite inviting. I watched as dragonflies played a game of tag above fields of grandfather's whiskers that swayed in the gentle breeze.

There was not much sign of human presence within the peaceful valley. At one point, a forest of tall old trees spanned both sides of the road. It felt reassuring knowing the army of green soldiers stood by strong and vigilant. Just a hoot-and-holler down the road was a quaint little town. No it wasn't Nirvana; it was Hell.

Despite its biblical connotations, the little town, population 266, was an unforgettable place. Although small in proportion to neighboring towns, the citizens were big on hospitality greeting one and all with a hardy, "Welcome to Hell!" or "How the hell are you?"

In 1836, George Reeves traveled from his home in New York and settled in Michigan.   In 1841, he built a saw mill on what became known as Hell Creek. He later purchased 1000 acres of land surrounding the mill. A gristmill was constructed to grind the grain for his distillery. Soon afterward, his neighbors were able to imbibe in these wares at his new tavern.

After the Civil War, tax collectors had come calling in search of lost revenues. George and his neighbors would hide the whiskey barrels by sinking them to the bottom of the mill pond. When the agents were gone, they hauled the barrels back up again.

Legend has it that when Michigan became a state, George was informed he needed to name his homestead. He replied with, "I don't care; you can just call it Hell for all I care!" They took him literally and the place would forever be known as Hell.

That day there was more than the usual amount of souls waiting to enter the Gates of Hell. It appeared Death had amassed quite a following as the 13th Annual Hearse Fest was under way. Hosted by a club known as Just Hearse'N Around, hearse enthusiasts would be proudly displaying their vehicles on the grounds. Later that day, there would be the annual parade with all the hearses flashing their lights and sounding the sirens for a less than somber procession. In 2011, they gained fame in the Guinness World Records as the largest hearse parade with a total of fifty-one vehicles.

Although I had investigated many places, the thought of communicating with spirit inside a hearse had never remotely occurred to me. Surely there was the possibility of a few souls that were still earthbound after taking their final ride. Or at least I might encounter some residual energy inside. Residual energy is something that imprints itself into other points of time and the scene plays itself over and over much like a movie. Sometimes it is the result of a traumatic event. What could be more so than a funeral? The loved ones and friends struggle to let go and say good bye. Likewise, the departed fearing the unknown of the afterlife may very well choose to linger and attempt to cling to familiar earthly surroundings.

Well, I need not have worried whether or not there would be activity. Because as usual, the word had gotten out that I would be going there. I swear it was as though my beacon was shining bright. *Hear ye! Hear ye, all you connected with one of the hearses, let your story be told! Now is your chance to speak.* And speak they did.

But for the life of me I could never understand why they chose to do this when I was driving. Sometimes it is very distracting to have a person pop up from the back seat and say, "Hey, I've got something to tell you!" Or worse yet is the annoying poking in the shoulder from the spirit that did not wish to wait their turn. Over time I had come to realize people did not instantly become angelic upon entering the afterlife. They still possessed the same personality and temperament as they did while on earth. Of course, that made our interactions all the more interesting.

As I neared my destination, the peacefulness of my ride was abruptly interrupted. The sobs of a grief-stricken woman brought me back to reality. She had short dark hair and was wearing a navy dress. Her face was pale and troubled. One hand held a handkerchief that gently wiped away the steady trickle of teardrops. The other gripped the strong hand of her husband. It seemed even the angels wept a quiet tear that day. She looked down at the small boy; a stuffed bear lay at his side. Sorrow crept up at the corners of her mouth. "Gone too soon," she cried. "Our little angel has gone too soon!"

Oh, my goodness. Didn't see that one coming! But before I could wrap my head around what the woman had just disclosed to me, another person was coming forward. Suddenly, I could hear the rustling of a line of souls gathering behind me. Then some of them began to push and shove their way to the front. *Sorry folks, but you're going to have to hold on until I get there. It's just up the road. And please, one at a time!*

As I entered the Gates of Hell, yes there was an actual sign over head, the sun sported a glaring stare. He had an unmistakably devilish grin as he called out, "Ha, ha welcome to hell, is it hot enough for you?"

Once inside there was no turning back. The energy was wickedly intense. I found myself in the midst of some of the most unique and amazing chariots of the dead; 64 to be exact. A few, a bit rusty, appeared as though they had risen from the ashes like a phoenix. Many of them had the most incredible and imaginative custom finishes. Others were adorned with a bevy of ghoulish accessories and, of course, devilish vanity plates; YURNEXT, LSTSTOP and LSTRYD were just a few. I couldn't wait to sit inside some of them and experience the energy.

Near the entrance, a soft spoken man tempted me to partake in a sip of his mysterious brew. Feeling like Eve in the garden, I found myself captivated surrendering to his devilish charms. As he lured me closer, the enticing aroma held me spellbound. How could I resist? In a mellow voice he whispered, "Trust me, this is sinfully good." Slowly I sipped the forbidden brew its shamefully seductive flavor lingering on my lips. Oh, how quickly I succumbed to the effects of those Deadly Grounds: Yes, it was the coffee to die for. *Where has this wondrous coffee been all my life?* As I savored every last drop, I noticed the vanity plate on their hearse and smiled: 2DIEFOR.

Slowly, I walked along the boulevard of broken dreams, unfinished business and forgotten souls. *Ok, here we are. You all wanted to talk to me while I was driving. Which one of these fine vehicles has a story to share? Now is your chance to tell me about your last ride.*

As I approached a green hearse, I felt a rush of total panic come over me. A teen age boy having slipped on the wet rocks lost his footing on the trail and plummeted into the raging river below. The water was icy cold. He screamed for help, but there was no one around to hear. The mighty current took its victim as it hurled his body to the depths below. He fought hard as the river attempted to strangle him. Although he could see the sunlight above him, his arms could not reach it. Muffled sounds of the world above filled his ears. The strength left his arms as the waters swallowed him up and he sank deeper into the dark abyss. Soon a soothing calmness came over him as he gave in and relinquished himself to the river.

Inside another hearse an older gentleman with faded blue eyes stood quietly at the cemetery. His face was etched with lines that seemed to carve out a map of his life. Ah life, he felt that life had stopped giving years ago and was now only taking away. And time was but a thief in the night taking his friends and now his beloved wife of sixty years. He laid her to rest in her favorite purple dress with the lace collar. Around her neck was the pearl necklace she had worn on their wedding day. As he stood there, the morning sun shined bright. It was as though everything would go on just fine without her, but how could it?

As I peered inside a black hearse, I could feel the heavy heart of a forty-something man wearing an Armani suit. He closed his eyes red and swollen after last night's deluge of memories streamed down his face. Men weren't supposed to cry. But his efforts were in vain as another lone tear managed to escape and trickle down past his quivering lips. It tasted salty yet bitter. He stared at the man's sun-kissed hair and then lingered on his face trying to memorize every detail; the arch of his eye brow, the dimple on his cheek and the contour of his chin. Slowly he reached for the hands of his beloved and slid his fingers over the gold band. Did he make a mistake telling the funeral director to leave it on? He glanced down at the matching ring on his finger and fumbled to slip it off. Tears began to well up again as he read the inscription inside: "Love never dies." His eyes moved back to his beloved's face and for a moment he thought he saw him smile. That was all the validation he needed.

The teenage boy looked on as mourners filed into the funeral home. He was not accustomed to wearing a suit, let alone a tie, but he didn't mind. Beautiful fragrant flowers surrounded the departed one. A small red spray with "son" and another with "grandson" were pinned to the lining of the casket. The woman's fingers trembled as she gently stroked her loved one's hair. He looked like an angel sleeping peacefully; ready to wake up at any moment. Oh, if only that were possible, she would never again complain about his messy room. It wasn't fair. Children weren't supposed to die before their mother. The girl with the long blonde hair fidgeted in her seat. She nervously picked at the angora yarn wrapped around the class ring too big for her slender finger. Her heart felt empty without him. Yet it was full of the first love they had shared. The boy in the suit felt so sorry for them. If only he knew how to consol them, he would. If only he could find the right words to say, he'd say them. If only he was able to wipe away their tears, he would do so. But he couldn't because he was the boy in the coffin.

Before I got totally overcome from all the tremendous emotional energy, I had to locate a special hearse. My friend Dave was the proud owner of a beautiful hearse he loving referred to as Ellie. Up ahead I spied her vanity plate which read GRAVEN1 referring to his art shop Graven Images Metalworks. I asked if I could have the honor of sitting down inside. What tales would she have to share with me?

I just barely slid inside and made myself comfortable when I heard, "Hey!" Then a hand gently touched my right arm. I was quite taken aback to see somebody sitting in the passenger seat; a man I could see right through. He was wearing a suit and dark cap. "How ya doin' Chief?" he asked. "Ridin' along with me?" He turned slightly and nodded his head toward the back. "This one will be takin' his last ride today," he said.

I looked over my shoulder to see an older portly man wearing a dark suit. If there would have been a way, he would have taken off that tie. His dear wife always insisted he wear one on special occasions. Since this was as special as you could get, he complied with her wishes one last time. She knelt down beside him and lovingly stroked his hand; the strong hand she had held for fifty years. He leaned in close to her ear and began to sing their song "Love Me Tender" in his best Elvis voice. Her trembling hand reached up to touch her ear. For just one moment, she almost smiled.

As I walked away, I was in awe with the memories that had been shared with me that day. An old song ran through my mind:

"But the ending always comes at last.
  Endings always come too fast.
  They come too fast, but they pass too slow.
  I love you and that's all I know."

--- Art Garfunkel

Just Hearse N' Around, Hell, MI

Deadly Grounds   www.deadlygroundscoffee.com

Dave & Ellie   www.gravenimagesmetalorks.com

Chapter 18

Beyond the Shadows

And so continues my amazing yet mysterious journey. Who else might I encounter from beyond the shadows along the way? How many more whispers from beyond the grave will I hear? What wondrous stories are they waiting to share with me? There is only one thing of which I am certain:

> "Sometimes the light's all shinin' on me.
> Other times I can barely see.
> Lately it occurs to me
> What a long, strange trip it's been."

> --- Grateful Dead